Communications in Computer and Information Science   **664**

Commenced Publication in 2007
Founding and Former Series Editors:
Alfredo Cuzzocrea, Dominik Ślęzak, and Xiaokang Yang

More information about this series at http://www.springer.com/series/7899

Zhang Zhang · Kaiqi Huang (Eds.)

Intelligent Visual Surveillance

4th Chinese Conference, IVS 2016
Beijing, China, October 19, 2016
Proceedings

 Springer

Editors
Zhang Zhang
Chinese Academy of Sciences
Beijing
China

Kaiqi Huang
Chinese Academy of Sciences
Beijing
China

ISSN 1865-0929   ISSN 1865-0937   (electronic)
Communications in Computer and Information Science
ISBN 978-981-10-3475-6   ISBN 978-981-10-3476-3   (eBook)
DOI 10.1007/978-981-10-3476-3

Library of Congress Control Number: 2016960565

Printed on acid-free paper

This Springer imprint is published by Springer Nature
The registered company is Springer Nature Singapore Pte Ltd.
The registered company address is: 152 Beach Road, #22-06/08 Gateway East, Singapore 189721, Singapore

Preface

Intelligent visual surveillance has emerged as a promising research area in computer vision. Intelligent visual surveillance has wide application perspective, and provides strong support for public security. To promote the adoption of visual surveillance, the previous three editions of the Chinese Conference on Intelligent Visual Surveillance were held in 2002, 2003, and 2011 successfully. In recent years, intelligent visual surveillance has experienced greater advancement. New solutions and techniques are being discovered continually. Furthermore, as more safe cities and smart cities have been constructed, the issues of public security have become much more important. And many surveillance companies are paying more attention to intelligent techniques in visual surveillance systems. In order to strengthen communication, enhance understanding, and improve cooperation between the academic and industrial communities, the 4th Chinese Conference on Intelligent Visual Surveillance (IVS 2016) was held on October 19, 2016.

After the call for papers was announced, we received 45 submissions covering all aspects of visual surveillance. The Technical Program Committee (TPC) assigned each submission to at least three reviewers with experience in the field of the submission. Then, the TPC member made decisions of acceptance/rejection based on the review reports. Through a rigid reviewing process, 19 papers were selected for this conference proceedings volume with an acceptance rate of 42.22%. The papers address the problems in object detection, motion tracking, person re-identification, action recognition, system architecture, and other related topics, and contribute new ideas to research and development of reliable and practical solutions for intelligent visual surveillance.

Finally, we would like to express our gratitude to all the contributors, reviewers, TPC and Organizing Committee members who made this a very successful conference. We also wish to acknowledge the Chinese Association for Artificial Intelligence, the Technical Committee on Computer Vision, China Computer Federation (CCF-CV), Springer, the Center for Research on Intelligent Perception and Computing, and the Institute of Automation for sponsoring this conference.

October 2016

Tieniu Tan
Shaogang Gong
Jake Aggarval

Organization

General Chairs

Tieniu Tan   Institute of Automation, CAS, China
Shaogang Gong   Queen Mary, University of London, UK
Jake Aggarval   The University of Texas at Austin, USA

Program Committee

Program Chairs

Kaiqi Huang   Institute of Automation, CAS, China
Chaowu Chen   First Research Institute of the Ministry of Public Security
                            of PRC, China
Dacheng Tao   University of Technology Sydney, Australia

Program Committee

Caifeng Shan   Philips Research, The Netherlands
Daoliang Tan   Beihang University, China
Dewen Hu   National University of Defense Technology, China
Grantham K.H. Pang   The University of Hong Kong, SAR China
Haizhou Ai   Tsinghua University, China
Hanzi Wang   Xiamen University, China
Huchuan Lu   Dalian University of Technology, China
Jianguo Zhang   University of Dundee, UK
Jianru Xue   Xi'an Jiaotong University, China
Jie Zhou   Tsinghua University, China
Jinfeng Yang   Civil Aviation University of China, China
Junge Zhang   Institute of Automation, CAS, China
Liang Lin   Sun Yat-sen University, China
Liang Wang   Institute of Automation, CAS, China
Lin Mei   Third Research Institute of the Ministry of Public Security
                            of PRC, China
Meibin Qi   Hefei University of Technology, China
Mingming Cheng   Nankai University, China
Rongrong Ji   Xiamen University, China
Shengjin Wang   Tsinghua University, China
Shiqi Yu   Shenzhen University, China
Shuai Zheng   Oxford University, UK
Stan Z. Li   Institute of Automation, CAS, China
Tiejun Huang   Peking University, China

Weiming Hu	Institute of Automation, CAS, China
Weishi Zheng	Sun Yat-sen University, China
Xiang Bai	Huazhong University of Science and Technology, China
Xiaogang Wang	Chinese University of Hong Kong, SAR China
Xiaokang Yang	Shanghai Jiao Tong University, China
Xiaotang Chen	Institute of Automation, CAS, China
Xiaoyi Jiang	University of Münster, Germany
Xin Zhao	Institute of Automation, CAS, China
Xuelong Li	Xi'an Institute of Optics and Precision Mechanics, CAS, China
Yunhong Wang	Beihang University, China
Yuxin Peng	Peking University, China
Zhang Zhang	Institute of Automation, CAS, China
Zhaoxiang Zhang	Institute of Automation, CAS, China
Zihe Fang	First Research Institute of the Ministry of Public Security of PRC, China

Organizers

Local Chair

Xin Zhao	Institute of Automation, CAS, China

Local Committee Members

Da Li	Institute of Automation, CAS, China
Dangwei Li	Institute of Automation, CAS, China
Jinde Liu	Institute of Automation, CAS, China
Qiaozhe Li	Institute of Automation, CAS, China
Ran Xu	Institute of Automation, CAS, China
Weihua Chen	Institute of Automation, CAS, China
Weiqi Zhao	Institute of Automation, CAS, China
Wenzhen Huang	Institute of Automation, CAS, China
Yabei Li	Institute of Automation, CAS, China
Yan Li	Institute of Automation, CAS, China
Yanhua Cheng	Institute of Automation, CAS, China
Yueyin Kao	Institute of Automation, CAS, China
Yupei Wang	Institute of Automation, CAS, China
Zhen Jia	Institute of Automation, CAS, China

CCF CV

Contents

Behavior, Activities, Crowd Analysis

Low-Level Preprocessing, Surveillance Systems

Occluded Object Imaging Based on Collaborative Synthetic Aperture Photography

Xiaoqiang Zhang[1($\boxtimes$)], Yanning Zhang[1], Tao Yang[1], Zhi Li[1], and Dapeng Tao[2]

[1] School of Computer Science and Engineering, Northwestern Polytechnical University, Xi'an, Shaanxi, People's Republic of China
vantasy@mail.nwpu.edu.cn
[2] School of Information Science and Engineering, Yunnan University, Kunming, People's Republic of China

Abstract. Occlusion poses as a critical challenge in computer vision for a long time. Camera array based synthetic aperture photography has been regarded as a promising way to address the problem of occluded object imaging. However, the application of this technique is limited by the building cost and the immobility of the camera array system. In order to build a more practical synthetic aperture photography system, in this paper, a novel multiple moving camera based collaborative synthetic aperture photography is proposed. The main characteristics of our work include: (1) to the best of our knowledge, this is the first multiple moving camera based collaborative synthetic aperture photography system; (2) by building a sparse 3D map of the occluded scene using one camera, the information from the subsequent cameras can be incrementally utilized to estimate the warping induced by the focal plane; (3) the compatibility of different types of cameras, such as the hand-held action cameras or the quadrotor on-board cameras, shows the generality of the proposed framework. Extensive experiments have demonstrated the see-through-occlusion performance of the proposed approach in different scenarios.

1 Introduction

In the field of computer vision, occlusions often impose significant challenges to various tasks, *e.g.* visual tracking and video surveillance. Since it is usually difficult to solve the occlusion problem from a single view, multiple views based approaches become a straightforward idea to solve the occlusion problem. Among the multi-view approaches, synthetic aperture photography (SAP) [1–7] provides plausible solutions to the occluded object imaging problems in a computational way. By warping and integrating images from different views, the multiple view system is computationally utilized to simulate a virtual camera with a very large synthetic aperture. Therefore, the depth of field of the synthetic image is so limited that the occluders, which are off the focal plane, would be blurred. Meanwhile the object, which is on the focal plane, would stay sharp (Fig. 1(c)). Thus, it provides the users the capability to see through occlusions.

© Springer Nature Singapore Pte Ltd. 2016
Z. Zhang and K. Huang (Eds.): IVS 2016, CCIS 664, pp. 3–11, 2016.
DOI: 10.1007/978-981-10-3476-3_1

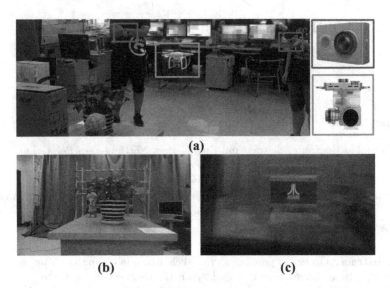

Fig. 1. Collaborative synthetic aperture photography system and occluded imaging result. (a) Collaborative data capturing. The occluded poster is collaboratively captured by different types of cameras: one on-board camera of a quadrotor (red box) and two action cameras (blue box). (b) The occluded scene. (c) Occluded object imaging result. (Color figure online)

Conventional SAP methods [1–3], utilize a camera array for the data capturing. However, the application of these approaches are limited due to the immobility and the high building cost of the array system and the inconvenience in system calibration. In the following works [4,5], a single moving camera is used to simulated a virtual camera array, which provides the users a more flexible way to generate the synthetic aperture images (SAIs). However, the camera motion is constrained in a line in [4]. Besides, in these approaches [4,5], if the SAI result is unsatisfied, the users need to re-capture the occluded object, discarding all previous captured information. Besides, both the two approaches cannot be applied to a multiple moving cameras based system. The lack of multiple moving cameras based SAP approach motivates us to consider the SAP problem in a collaborative way. That is, rather than a single moving camera, multiple moving cameras, even in different types, can be used to collaboratively capture the scene and generate the synthetic aperture images. As shown in Fig. 1(b), in the scene, a planar poster is occluded by a potted plant and other objects. Images captured by different types of cameras, including the on-board camera of a quadrotor and action cameras (Fig. 1(a)), are collaboratively utilized to generate the see-through-occlusion imaging result, which is shown in Fig. 1(c). To the best of our knowledge, the proposed method is the first time to solve the occluded object imaging problem within a collaborative multiple moving cameras framework.

In the SAP technique, images from different cameras or views are warped onto a virtual focal plane. Hence, one of the core problems of the SAP is the estimation of the transformation matrices used in the warping. In the conventional camera array based methods [1–3], the estimation is done by an offline calibration procedure. However in our case, the estimation is more challenging since multiple moving cameras of different types are utilized in our system. Inspired by the bag-of-words [8] based place recognition approaches [9–11], in this paper, a novel multiple collaborative framework is proposed to estimate of the transformations used when generating the SAIs. In this framework, one selected camera is used to build a sparse map of the occluded scene, which is then collaboratively utilized to incrementally estimate the poses of the images from the subsequent cameras. Finally, with the user specified focal plane, the synthetic aperture image are generated by warping images from all cameras onto the focal plane. Compared to the previous single moving camera based approaches [4,5], the proposed method can provide a SAP approach for multiple users. Moreover, if the SAI result is unsatisfied, the users can incrementally capture the same scene from different perspectives, without discarding the previous captured information. Experimental results on datasets captured both indoor and outdoor demonstrate the performance of our approach.

2 Collaborative Synthetic Aperture Photography

In this section, we describe the details of the proposed collaborative SAP method. The pipeline of the proposed method is illustrated in Fig. 2.

• **System Overview.** As shown in Fig. 2, cameras used in our system are divided into two types: one main camera (red dashed box in Fig. 2) and several sub cameras (blue dashed box in Fig. 2). In our collaborative framework, the main camera is set to capture an image sequence of a scene and m frames will be selected for the SAI generation, which are denoted as $I_{K1}, \ldots, I_{Km}$. And the sub cameras are set to capture images from different perspectives. Here we suppose there are L sub cameras in total. For the j-th sub camera, it captures N_j images in total. Mathematically, The SAI, I_{sa}, can be represented by

$$I_{sa} = \frac{1}{m + \sum_{j=1}^{L} N_j} \left(\sum_{i=1}^{m} P(M_i, I_{Ki}) + \sum_{j=1}^{L} \sum_{k=1}^{N_j} P(M_{jk}, I_{jk}) \right), \quad (1)$$

where M denotes the transformation matrix that projects the corresponding image onto the focal plane, I_{jk} the k-th image captured from sub camera j and $P(\cdot, \cdot)$ the required projection procedure. Usually, M is determined by the pose of the corresponding image and the focal plane. In this section, the main focus is the collaborative pose estimation.

As shown in Fig. 2, there are four main steps in the proposed approach. Firstly, one camera is selected as the main camera, and the sparse 3D map of the occluded scene is estimated from the image sequence captured by the main camera via a keyframe-based SLAM approach. During the SLAM, image features and their descriptors on a certain keyframe, are converted into a bag-of-words

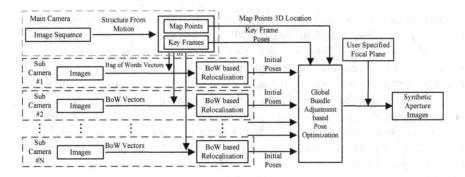

Fig. 2. Framework of the proposed collaborative SAP method. (Color figure online)

(BoW) vector. The keyframes and its BoW vector, as well as the estimated sparse 3D map of the scene, are stored for the next step. Secondly, in order to obtain more information of the occluded object, several sub cameras are used to capture the scene from perspectives that are different from those of the keyframes from the main camera. The pose of each image from each sub camera are initially estimated via BoW based relocalisation, in which the sparse map and keyframe BoW vectors obtained from the first step are utilized. Thirdly, the pose of all keyframes of the main camera, and that of all images from all sub cameras are optimized via a global bundle adjustment. Finally, with the user specified focal plane, the induced warping can be computed and the synthetic aperture image is generated.

• **Keyframe-Based SLAM for the Main Camera.** In this step, we take the image sequence captured from the main camera as the input. Because the goal of our system is to estimate the poses of frames from different camera, in this step, we choose to adopt the work of ORB-SLAM [11] for its convenience when performing relocalisation. For the completeness, a brief review of the related procedure is given below. More formal descriptions are given in [10,11].

The ORB-SLAM follows the traditional pipeline of the keyframe-based SLAM approaches. The ORB feature descriptor is selected for the feature tracking and mapping procedure. During the SLAM, for each selected keyframe, the extracted ORB features are converted into a bag-of-words vector, and stored in a pre-trained visual vocabulary tree, which can be used for the relocalisation in the following step. As well, the 3D locations of the estimated sparse map points are stored.

• **Sub Camera Pose Estimation via Relocalisation.** In this step, the goal is to estimate the poses of each image of each sub camera. Suppose an image, I_{it}, is the t-th captured image from sub camera i. Because the scene is sparsely sampled by the keyframes from the main camera, I_{it} would share some similarities with some of the keyframes, which can be measured by the similarity between the two bag-of-words vectors [9]. It can be defined as

$$s(v_{it}, v_{Kj}) = 1 - \frac{1}{2} \left| \frac{v_{it}}{|v_{it}|} - \frac{v_{Kj}}{|v_{Kj}|} \right|, \tag{2}$$

where v_{it} and v_{Kj} are, respectively, the bag-of-words vectors of I_{it} and that of the j-th keyframe from the main camera. Therefore, by calculating and sorting the similarity score (Eq. (2)) between I_{it} and all keyframes, the keyframe that shares the most similarities with I_{it}, which is represented by I_{Kit}, can be retrieved and will be used to estimate the pose of I_{it}.

Since I_{Kit} is the keyframe obtained from the first step, its feature points are associated with the 3D map points, we can establish the 2D-3D correspondences between image features on I_{it} and the map points by computing the 2D-2D pixel correspondences between I_{it} and I_{Kit}. Then, with the 2D-3D correspondences, the pose of I_{it} can be estimated by solving the Perspective-n-Point (PnP) using [12] or the UPnP problem [13], depending on sub camera i is calibrated or not. In practice, considering the mismatching situation and outliers of the map point, the RANSAC scheme is used when estimating the pose of I_{it}. This step is continued until the pose of all images from all sub cameras are estimated. If the RANSAC scheme fails when estimating the pose, the corresponding image will be discard when generating the SAI.

Finally, the pose of all keyframes from the main camera, and those of all the images from all sub cameras, are optimized via a global bundle adjustment. It should be noted that the proposed collaborative framework also works for other SfM or relocalisation approaches. Therefore, the SfM and relocalisation approaches are not specified in Fig. 2.

• **Synthetic Aperture Image Generation.** Before generating the SAI, one view, either from the main camera or from the sub cameras, is selected as a reference view. The SAI will be generated in the camera coordinate system of the reference view. Without loss of generality, in practice, we usually select the first keyframe as the reference view.

Suppose that the coordinate of the focal plane Π is $(\mathbf{n}^\top, d)^\top$, in which $\mathbf{n}^\top$ is the normal vector of Π and d a scalar. With the abuse of the notations, we use M_i to represent the transformation matrix that projects the corresponding image I_i onto the focal plane. Geometrically, M_i is the homography induced by Π between I_i and the reference view I_{ref}, and can be computed by

$$M_i = K_i(R_i - \mathbf{t_i}\mathbf{n}^\top/d)K_{ref}, \tag{3}$$

where K_i and K_{ref} are, respectively, the intrinsic parameter matrix of I_i and I_{ref}, R_i and $\mathbf{t_i}$ the relative rotation and translation between I_i and I_{ref}.

After estimating all the induced warping for all images, the SAI is generated using Eq. (1).

3 Experimental Results

In this section, we describe the details of the experimental results to show the performance of the proposed occluded object imaging method.

Fig. 3. Occluded object imaging result indoor. (a) The reference view of the occluded scene. (b) A sample image from the sub camera. (c) The SAI generated using only keyframes from the main camera. (d) The SAI generated using the proposed collaborative framework.

- **Equipment.** One of the main features of the proposed collaborative SAP method is that different types of cameras can be used in the framework. In order to show the generality of the proposed method, we choose to use several on-the-shelf cameras of different types for data capturing in the experiments. Moreover, to show the application of the proposed method on aerial videos, the on-board camera of a quadrotor is also utilized. In particular, for the quadrotor, the DJI phantom 4, which is a high-end but affordable quadrotor with good on-board camera, is selected. For the other cameras, several Yi action cameras are used. The two types of camera are both shown in Fig. 1. Before the data capturing, the intrinsic parameter of these cameras are set to be fixed and calibrated. The captured image sequences from these cameras are uploaded to a desktop with an Intel Core i5-4460 CPU @3.2GHz. We develop a C++ based system to generate the SAIs using the proposed collaborative system.

Considering the fact that the depth-of-field of the SAI is very limited, it is difficult to get the entire non-planar object in focus. In the following experiments, we choose to use planar object to be the imaging object.

- **Exp. A. Occluded Poster in an Indoor Scene.** In this experiment, our goal is to demonstrate the performance of the proposed method in the indoor scene. As shown in Fig. 3(a), in the scene, a planar poster is severely occluded by a potted plant and a toy doll. During the data capturing, the on-board camera of DJI phantom 4 is selected as the main camera. Since the main goal of the main camera is to build the sparse map of the scene, it is set to work at lower resolution but high frame rate mode. In this experiment, the main camera captures images sequence with a resolution of 1280×720 pixels at 50 fps using a frontal perspective. Two Yi action cameras are used as the sub cameras in this experiment. They both captures images with a resolution of 1920×1080 pixels, which shares the same aspect ratio with that of the main camera. Figure 3(a) shows the reference view, which is the first keyframe out of all 13 keyframes selected from the main camera. In total, 50 frames are captured from the two sub cameras. One sample image is shown in Fig. 3(b).

Figure 3(c) and (d) show, respectively, the occluded object imaging result using all keyframes and all images in our collaborative system. In SLAM approaches, the keyframe selection criterion are usually based on the number of successful tracked map points, rather than enhancement the occluded object imaging performance. Besides, because the indoor scene is small, during the SLAM, not many keyframes are selected. Figure 3(c) provides only partial information of the occluded poster. However in the proposed collaborative method, because two sub cameras are utilized to capture extra information of the occluded object, the SAI result in Fig. 3(d) are more clearer see-through-occlusion imaging result.

- **Exp. B. Outdoor Experiment Using Aerial Images from Multiple Flights.** Considering the scene scale is small indoor, an outdoor experiment is conducted to further demonstrate the performance of the proposed method. As shown in Fig. 4(a), a planar poster is occluded by a metal trolley. Considering that the scene is difficult to capture from hand-held cameras, we incrementally capture the scene from several flights. Image sequence captured in the first flight are used to build the sparse map of the scene, while the subsequent flights provide more detailed information of the occluded object.

Different from the previous experiment, the quadrotor is controlled to capture images from top-down perspectives. The on-board camera is set to capture images with a resolution of 1280×720 pixels and image sequence at 50 fps for the first flight. During the experiment, we conduct 3 flights with different heights ranging from 2 to 3 m. It should be noted that the occlusion-to-object distance in this experiment is only 0.15 m, which makes it more challenging to remove of the occlusions. Figure 4(b) shows the reference view, which is captured during the first flight. Figure 4(c) shows the SAI result generated from 35 images. It

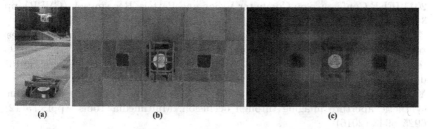

(a)   (b)   (c)

Fig. 4. Occluded object imaging result outdoor. (a) The DJI phantom 4 are used to incrementally capture the occluded poster from a top-down perspective. (b) The reference view. (c) The occluded object imaging result.

can be seen that the entire pattern of the occluded poster can be seen in the SAI and the occluded is blurred out. This experiment shows that the proposed method can also be used for aerial video based occluded object imaging.

4   Conclusion

In this work, a novel multiple moving camera based collaborative SAP method is proposed. In this framework, one selected camera is used to build a sparse map of the occluded scene, which is then collaboratively utilized to incrementally estimate the poses of the images from the subsequent cameras. Experiment from indoor and outdoor scene and captured by both quadrotors and hand-held camera demonstrate the performance and the generality of the proposed approaches. In the future work, we would like to extend the propose method to build a multiple quadrotors based occluded object imaging system.

Acknowledgments. This work is supported the National Natural Science Foundation of China (No. 61272288, No. 61301192, No. 61303123, No. 61672429, No. 61231016 (Key Project)), NPU New People and New Directions Foundation (No.1 3GH014604), The Fundamental Research Funds for the Central Universities (No. 3102015AX007), NPU New Ao Xiang Star (No. G2015KY0301), and Shen Zhen Science and Technology Foundation (JCYJ20160229172932237).

References

1. Vaish, V., Wilburn, B., Joshi, N., Levoy, M.: Using plane+ parallax for calibrating dense camera arrays. In: Proceedings of the 2004 IEEE Computer Society Conference on Computer Vision and Pattern Recognition, CVPR 2004, vol. 1, p. I-2. IEEE (2004)
2. Vaish, V., Garg, G., Talvala, E.V., Antunez, E., Wilburn, B., Horowitz, M., Levoy, M.: Synthetic aperture focusing using a shear-warp factorization of the viewing transform. In: IEEE Computer Society Conference on Computer Vision and Pattern Recognition-Workshops, CVPR Workshops, p. 129. IEEE (2005)
3. Yang, T., Zhang, Y., Tong, X., Zhang, X., Yu, R.: Continuously tracking and see-through occlusion based on a new hybrid synthetic aperture imaging model. In: 2011 IEEE Conference on Computer Vision and Pattern Recognition (CVPR), pp. 3409–3416. IEEE (2011)
4. Zhang, X., Zhang, Y., Yang, T., Song, Z.: Calibrate a moving camera on a linear translating stage using virtual plane + parallax. In: Yang, J., Fang, F., Sun, C. (eds.) IScIDE 2012. LNCS, vol. 7751, pp. 48–55. Springer, Heidelberg (2013). doi:10.1007/978-3-642-36669-7_7
5. Yang, T., Ma, W., Wang, S., Li, J., Yu, J., Zhang, Y.: Kinect based real-time synthetic aperture imaging through occlusion. Multimedia Tools Appl. **75**(12), 6925–6943 (2016)
6. Yang, T., Zhang, Y., Yu, J., Li, J., Ma, W., Tong, X., Yu, R., Ran, L.: All-in-focus synthetic aperture imaging. In: Fleet, D., Pajdla, T., Schiele, B., Tuytelaars, T. (eds.) ECCV 2014. LNCS, vol. 8694, pp. 1–15. Springer, Cham (2014). doi:10.1007/978-3-319-10599-4_1

7. Zhang, X., Zhang, Y., Yang, T., Yang, Y.H.: Synthetic aperture photography using a moving camera-IMU system. Pattern Recogn. **62**, 175–188 (2017)
8. Nister, D., Stewenius, H.: Scalable recognition with a vocabulary tree. In: 2006 IEEE Computer Society Conference on Computer Vision and Pattern Recognition, vol. 2, pp. 2161–2168. IEEE (2006)
9. Gálvez-López, D., Tardos, J.D.: Bags of binary words for fast place recognition in image sequences. IEEE Trans. Robot. **28**, 1188–1197 (2012)
10. Mur-Artal, R., Tardós, J.D.: Fast relocalisation and loop closing in keyframe-based SLAM. In: 2014 IEEE International Conference on Robotics and Automation (ICRA), pp. 846–853. IEEE (2014)
11. Mur-Artal, R., Montiel, J., Tardós, J.D.: ORB-SLAM: a versatile and accurate monocular SLAM system. IEEE Trans. Robot. **31**, 1147–1163 (2015)
12. Lepetit, V., Moreno-Noguer, F., Fua, P.: EPnP: an accurate $o(n)$ solution to the PnP problem. Int. J. Comput. Vis. **81**, 155–166 (2009)
13. Penate-Sanchez, A., Andrade-Cetto, J., Moreno-Noguer, F.: Exhaustive linearization for robust camera pose and focal length estimation. IEEE Trans. Pattern Anal. Mach. Intell. **35**, 2387–2400 (2013)

Video Synchronization with Trajectory Pulse

Xue Wang[✉] and Qing Wang

School of Computer, Northwestern Polytechnical University,
Xi'an 710072, People's Republic of China
xwang@mail.nwpu.edu.cn

Abstract. This paper presents a method to temporally synchronize two independently moving cameras with overlapping views. Temporal variations between image frames (such as moving objects) are powerful cues for alignment. We first generate pulse images by tracking moving objects and examining the trajectories for changes in speed. We then integrate a rank-based constraint and the pulse-based matching, to derive a robust approximation of spatio-temporal alignment quality for all pairs of frames. By folding both spatial and temporal cues into a single alignment framework, finally, the nonlinear temporal mapping is found using a graph-based approach that supports partial temporal overlap between sequences. We verify the robustness and performance of the proposed approach on several challenging real video sequences. Compared to state-of-the-art techniques, our approach is robust to tracking error and can handle non-rigid scene alignment in complex dynamic scenes.

1 Introduction

Video synchronization is part of a more general video alignment problem which occurs in tasks such as human motion recognition, video retrieval, multi-view surveillance and 3D visualization. Videos must be aligned both spatially and temporally. Spatial alignment computes the geometrical transformation of 2D or 3D coordinate systems of temporally aligned frames, so that the object of interest is in correspondence. Temporal alignment computes 1D temporal transformation by synchronizing frames to achieve good spatial alignment.

Jointly reasoning about temporal and spatial alignment improves the robustness of the system. There are two main challenges. First, explicit 2D or 3D spatial alignment is very difficult to compute for moving cameras on dynamically changing scene with multiple moving objects. Second, due to non-predictable frame drops, temporal context constraints (i.e. continuity) can not be applied everywhere for temporal alignment.

The key insight is the spatio-temporal rhythm of movement of a human body. Both the geometrical configuration and the speed variations of body parts, are strong cues for alignment. Furthermore, the body configuration and movement are often coupled. Our method uses sparse space-time point trajectories as input.

This work was partially supported by National Natural Science Foundation of China (61272287, 61531014).

Z. Zhang and K. Huang (Eds.): IVS 2016, CCIS 664, pp. 12–19, 2016.
DOI: 10.1007/978-981-10-3476-3_2

We introduce a temporal feature, *pulse*, along each trajectory by examining the changes in speed. We call this feature *pulse* as it reflects the rhythm of movement, also the peaks and troughs on a *pulse* image are often associated with the keyframes of body poses. With the *pulse* features, our objective is to measure the sequence-to-sequence alignment quality between pairs of frames with a gross approximation of synchronization (i.e., constant offset model). On the other hand, following traditional image-to-image alignment techniques, we measure the spatial configuration alignment between two camera frames using a rank constraint based on epipolar geometry. This implicitly considers 3D transformation without solving a hard reconstruction problem. Finally we fold both the *pulse* based matching and the rank constraint into a single alignment framework, and compute the globally optimal path that minimizes spatial and temporal misalignments.

2   Related Works

Most video alignment techniques assume stationary or rigidly fixed cameras, thus a fixed spatial transformation between corresponding frames is guaranteed and need not be re-estimated at runtime. Commonly exploited geometric constraints include plane-induced homography [1,2], affine transformation [3], binocular epipolar geometry constraint [1,4,5], deficient rank conditions arose from special projection models [6–8] and so on. Anthony et al. [9] propose to synchronize stationary cameras using inflection points, which are found by examining the trajectories for changes in direction. Once an event has been identified in two such videos, a temporal mapping between the sequences can be globally described by simple parametric models, like constant offset model [2,4,6,7] or 1D affine model [1,5,8]. Nonlinear temporal mapping is used to cope with free form of time correspondence [3,10]. Assuming simultaneous recording, this kind of temporal rigidity is preserved even for independently moving cameras [11–14]. If related videos are captured at different points in time, previous work [15–18] assumes approximately coincident camera trajectories, to make sure that corresponding frames are captured from similar viewpoints.

Our scenario is most closely related to the work in [11–14], which focuses on video alignment for independently moving cameras and non-rigid dynamic scenes. Tresadern and Reid [11] develop a unified rank constraint framework for homography, perspective and affine projection models. Tuytelaars and Gool [12] assume a scaled orthographic projection model and find corresponding frames use the line-to-line distance of the back-projection 3D lines of matching points. Lei and Yang [14] use the tri-ocular geometric constraint of point/line features to build the timeline maps for multiple sequences. These methods assume that the features are tracked successfully throughout each sequence and matched across sequences, which are hardly assured in wide baseline conditions. Also they try to recover a linear synchronization. Dexter et al. [13] propose a time-adaptive descriptor based on self-similarity matrices to perform nonlinear synchronization. However, they use static points in the background to estimate a dominant motion to compensate modest camera motion, which only works for distant views or planar scenes.

3   Trajectory Pulse

Let $F = \{\mathbf{x}_1, \mathbf{x}_2, \ldots, \mathbf{x}_M\}$ and $F' = \{\mathbf{x}'_1, \mathbf{x}'_2, \ldots, \mathbf{x}'_N\}$ denote two corresponding feature trajectories from video sequences M and N frames long respectively. Both sequences have a collection of feature trajectories $\Gamma = (F^1, F^2, \ldots, F^K)$ and $\Gamma' = (F'^1, F'^2, \ldots, F'^K)$, with K the number of trajectories for both sequences. Let $v_i(j)$ denote the jth frame of video i. Our goal is to find a nonlinear temporal mapping $\mathbf{p} : \mathbb{N} \rightarrow \mathbb{N}$, where $\mathbf{p}(n) = m$ maps $v_1(m)$ in the reference sequence to $v_2(n)$ in the observed sequence. Considering the situation that the temporal displacements are not necessarily integer values, instead of a sub-frame accurate synchronization, we find the temporally closest frame.

Given two sets of corresponding trajectories Γ and Γ', there are two ways of looking at the spatio-temporal alignment. To represent the time varying structure in the trajectory space, between two corresponding point trajectories F and F', a temporal trajectory affinity across views can be used for temporal synchronization. To represent the time varying structure in the shape space, between two instantaneous 2D point configurations $(\mathbf{x}_m^1, \mathbf{x}_m^2, \ldots, \mathbf{x}_m^K)$ and $(\mathbf{x}_n'^1, \mathbf{x}_n'^2, \ldots, \mathbf{x}_n'^K)$, a spatial shape affinity across views can also be used. Thus a best match should have both high temporal trajectory affinity and high spatial shape affinity.

We generate pulse images by examining the trajectories for changes in speed, which reflects how fast the instantaneous point velocity changes. The frames where the speed changes drastically can be seen as the pulse feature for temporal alignment. Two examples of pulse images for corresponding trajectories are given in Fig. 1. Each pulse image has been normalized to zero mean. The trajectories of torso, whose variances are 1.62 and 2.43 respectively, lack distinctive pulse features so that multiple temporal mappings can align the two trajectories. While the trajectories of left hand, whose variances are 16.32 and 9.08 respectively, provide discriminative pulse features to determine a unique solution for temporal alignment.

The conclusions accord with the general impression. A static object contributes nothing for video alignment. In general, greater temporal variations a dynamic scene the better chances of exact video synchronization. The pulse feature with obvious change in speed provides powerful alignment cues. Once we have generated the pulse images for the corresponding trajectories, for each feasible pair of frames, the synchronization is grossly determined by the frames using a constant offset model. Accordingly the pulse-based trajectory affinity $\mathbf{A}_t$ for frame pair (m, n) is defined as follows,

$$\mathbf{A}_t(m, n) = \exp(-\frac{trj_{m,n}}{\sigma_t^2}), \qquad (1)$$

where $trj_{m,n}$ is the maximum pulse images difference for corresponding trajectories, and σ_t is a positive rate.

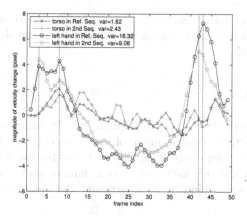

Fig. 1. Two examples of pulse images for corresponding trajectories. The discriminative pulse features are indicated in black dotted vertical lines.

4   Nonlinear Temporal Alignment

For perspective projection model, given K corresponding points, the unknown fundamental matrix $\mathbf{F}$ can be computed using $\mathbf{Mf} = 0$, where $\mathbf{M}$ is a $K \times 9$ observation matrix of constraints defined by the image feature locations, $\mathbf{f}$ is the elements of the fundamental matrix: $\mathbf{f} = [f_1, \ldots, f_8, 1]^\top$ [11]. Since it is a homogenous equation, for a solution of $\mathbf{f}$ to exist, $\mathbf{M}$ must have rank at most eight. However, due to the noise or the tracking error, the rank of $\mathbf{M}$ will almost always be of full rank. We examine the *effective rank*, $\hat{n}$, of the observation matrix [7]. Let $\lambda_1, \ldots, \lambda_h$ denote the singular values of $\mathbf{M}$. The sum of remaining singular values, denoted as $dst = \sum_{k=\hat{n}+1}^{h} \lambda_k$, can be used to measure the matching of two instantaneous 2D point configurations. The smallest dst of $\mathbf{M}$ corresponds to the best match of frames. Finally, we transform dst to the shape affinity $\mathbf{A}_s(m, n)$ as follows,

$$\mathbf{A}_s(m, n) = \exp(-\frac{dst_{m,n}}{\sigma_s^2}). \tag{2}$$

where σ_s is a positive rate. Thus we set the spatio-temporal affinity $\mathbf{A}(m, n)$ for frame pair (m, n) by integrating the shape and trajectory affinity,

$$\mathbf{A}(m, n) = \exp\left[-(\frac{dst_{m,n}}{\sigma_s^2} + \frac{trj_{m,n}}{\sigma_t^2})\right]. \tag{3}$$

where σ_t and σ_s control the rate of decay for trajectory and shape weights respectively. Finally, we transform the $\mathbf{A}$ to obtain the cost matrix $\mathbf{C}$ in which low values indicate frames that are likely to have a *good* match. The entries of the cost matrix $\mathbf{C}$ are given by,

$$\mathbf{C}(m, n) = 1 - \frac{\mathbf{A}(m, n)}{\mathbf{A}_{max}}, \tag{4}$$

where $\mathbf{A}_{max}$ is the maximum value of $\mathbf{A}$.

The nonlinear temporal mapping $\mathbf{p} : \mathbb{N} \to \mathbb{N}$ is referred as a path through the cost matrix. We use the mapping computing algorithm described in [16] to find the optimal path.

5   Experiments

In this section, we evaluate the proposed alignment algorithm on several channeling real data. We focus on the alignment of sequences captured by independently moving cameras simultaneously from different viewpoints. The corresponding feature trajectories are the joint points in a human body labelled manually. When some points are occluded, we interpolate the missing locations between consecutive frames.

We perform an ablative analysis of our approach, by comparing to the following baselines: (1) using trajectory affinity $\mathbf{A}_t$ alone of Eq. 1, and (2) using shape affinity $\mathbf{A}_s$ alone of Eq. 2. We additionally compare our approach with three state-of-the-art synchronization algorithms for independently moving cameras [12,13,16], abbreviated as BPM, MFM and SMM, respectively.

Given the ground truth $\{\hat{\mathbf{p}}(j), j)\}_{j=1...M}$, we use the average absolute temporal alignment error $\varepsilon = \frac{1}{M} \sum_{j=1}^{M} |\hat{\mathbf{p}}(j) - \mathbf{p}(j)|$ as our basic accuracy metric.

5.1   Non-rigid Scene Alignment

For evaluation with videos captured with independently moving simultaneously, we first use the *Fight* dataset provided by [19]. Further, we introduce a first-person dataset captured by heal-mounted cameras, which consists of three social interaction scenes. The scenes, *Blocks* and *Exercise mat*, capture tetradic interactions between children aged 5–6. For the *Basketball* scene, the players strategically take advantage of team formation (5v5). Ground truth are obtained by manual synchronization. We take two clips with temporal overlapping for alignment. Within the observed sequence, we drop several frames randomly at a maximum rate 5%.

The average temporal alignment errors with respect to the ground truth are summarized in Table 1. The complete model of our approach outperforms other methods on the test sequences. The content-based snapping [16] assumes that two frames are more likely to be "alignable" if they contain a large number of similar features, and it is unable to accurately synchronize sequences in the wide baseline viewing condition.

Figure 2 shows the synchronization results for sample frames using the complete model of our approach, BPM, MFM and SMM on different scenes. Three alignment situations are defined according to the alignment accuracies. For a frame $v_i(j)$, its alignment error is defined as $\varepsilon_j = |\hat{\mathbf{p}}(j) - \mathbf{p}(j)|$. Thus, the frame $v_i(j)$ is referred as a *matched, slightly mismatched* or *mismatched* frame when $\varepsilon_j \leq 1$, $\varepsilon_j \leq 2$ and $\varepsilon_j \geq 3$, respectively.

Table 1. Comparisons of alignment error for non-rigid scene alignment.

	Fight	*Blocks*	*Exercise mat*	*Basketball*
BPM [12]	12.6	24.7	15.1	22.3
MFM [13]	4.9	14.2	16.8	9.4
SMM [16]	18.7	138.5	106.9	19.1
Our method (shape)	8.1	17.0	30.7	15.3
Our method (trajectory)	2.5	13.6	8.4	3.7
Our method (complete)	**1.2**	**1.6**	**2.5**	**0.8**

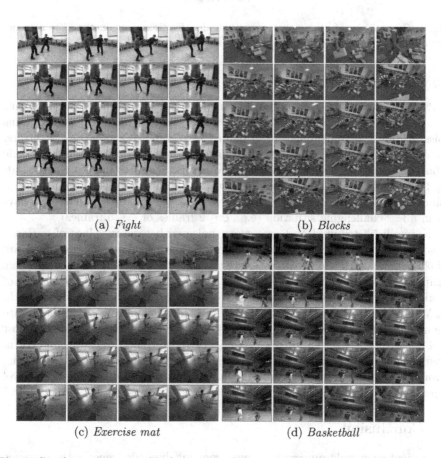

(a) *Fight*   (b) *Blocks*

(c) *Exercise mat*   (d) *Basketball*

Fig. 2. Synchronization results for sample frames on different scenes. *From top to bottom*: Sample frames from the reference sequence, corresponding frames from the observed sequence by the complete model of our method, BPM, MFM and SMM. The red, yellow and green rectangles around the frames indicate *matched*, *slightly mismatched* and *mismatched* frames, respectively. (Color figure online)

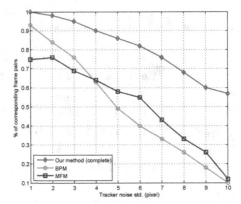

Fig. 3. Comparison of alignment error versus localization error on the *Blocks* scene. The alignment error bound is fixed at $\zeta = 1$ frame.

5.2 Robustness Analysis

Feature-based methods rely on the point trajectories as input data for alignment. In a practical situation, the feature trajectory is usually imperfect and contains noise. A robust alignment algorithm should be tolerate to certain tracking errors. We evaluate the effect of noisy trajectories on the proposed approach using the robustness analysis [3,5]. We consider the percentage of estimated corresponding frame pairs below a given bound ζ, which allows us to assess the algorithm robustness to compute high-accurate timelines ($\zeta \leq 1$ frame) as well as its behavior in a less challenging situation (e.g., $\zeta \leq 2$ frames or $\zeta \leq 5$ frames).

Normally distributed and zero mean noise with various values of variance is added to the tracked feature trajectories. The original point locations are labelled manually. Then we can estimate the algorithm by computing the average temporal alignment error in a variety of settings. Figure 3 shows the impact of localization error on alignment accuracy for the complete model of our approach, BPM and MFM on the *Blocks* scene. As expected, the ability to achieve accurate alignments diminishes with increased noise levels. Our approach can align almost 80% of the total frames within a ±1 frame offset with respect to the ground truth, even when the tracker noise variance reaches 6. Due to the sensitivity to tracking error, previous methods deteriorate at a faster rate as the tracking noise level increases comparing to ours.

6 Conclusion

We present a general framework for synchronizing dynamic scenes in the presence of independent camera motion. We demonstrate the feasibility of folding pulse-based trajectory affinity and rank-based shape affinity into a single alignment framework. Experiments conducted on several challenging video sequences show that the proposed approach outperforms the synchronization accuracy and the robustness w.r.t the state-of-the-art techniques.

References

1. Caspi, Y., Simakov, D., Irani, M.: Feature-based sequence-to-sequence matching. Int. J. Comput. Vis. **68**, 53–64 (2006)
2. Dai, C., Zheng, Y., Li, X.: Accurate video alignment using phase correlation. IEEE Signal Process. Lett. **13**(12), 737–740 (2006)
3. Lu, C., Mandal, M.: A robust technique for motion-based video sequences temporal alignment. IEEE Trans. Multimedia **15**, 70–82 (2013)
4. Pundik, D., Moses, Y.: Video synchronization using temporal signals from epipolar lines. In: Daniilidis, K., Maragos, P., Paragios, N. (eds.) ECCV 2010. LNCS, vol. 6313, pp. 15–28. Springer, Heidelberg (2010). doi:10.1007/978-3-642-15558-1_2
5. Pádua, F., Carceroni, R., Santos, G., Kutulakos, K.: Linear sequence-to-sequence alignment. IEEE Trans. Pattern Anal. Mach. Intell. **32**, 304–320 (2010)
6. Wolf, L., Zomet, A.: Correspondence-free synchronization and reconstruction in a non-rigid scene. In: Workshop on Vision and Modelling of Dynamic Scenes (2002)
7. Wolf, L., Zomet, A.: Wide baseline matching between unsynchronized video sequences. Int. J. Comput. Vis. **68**, 43–52 (2006)
8. Rao, C., Gritai, A., Shah, M., Syeda-Mahmood, T.: View-invariant alignment and matching of video sequences. In: International Conference on Computer Vision (2003)
9. Whitehead, A., Laganiere, R., Bose, P.: Temporal synchronization of video sequences in theory and in practice. In: Applications of Computer Vision and the IEEE Workshop on Motion and Video Computing, pp. 132–137(2005)
10. Singh, M., Cheng, I., Mandal, M., Basu, A.: Optimization of symmetric transfer error for sub-frame video synchronization. In: Forsyth, D., Torr, P., Zisserman, A. (eds.) ECCV 2008. LNCS, vol. 5303, pp. 554–567. Springer, Heidelberg (2008). doi:10.1007/978-3-540-88688-4_41
11. Tresadern, P.A., Reid, I.D.: Video synchronization from human motion using rank constraints. Comput. Vis. Image Underst. **113**, 891–906 (2009)
12. Tuytelaars, T., Gool, L.V.: Synchronizing video sequences. In: IEEE Computer Society Conference on Computer Vision and Pattern Recognition (2004)
13. Dexter, E., Pérez, P., Laptev, I.: Multi-view synchronization of human actions and dynamic scenes. In: Proceedings of the British Machine Vision Conference (2009)
14. Lei, C., Yang, Y.: Trifocal tensor-based multiple video synchronization with sub-frame optimization. IEEE Trans. Image Process. **15**, 2473–2480 (2006)
15. Evangelidis, G., Bauckhage, C.: Efficient subframe video alignment using short descriptors. IEEE Trans. Pattern Anal. Mach. Intell. **35**, 2371–2386 (2013)
16. Wang, O., Schroers, C., Zimmer, H., Gross, M., Sorkine-Hornung, A.: Videosnapping: interactive synchronization of multiple videos. In: SIGGRAPH (2014)
17. Diego, F., Ponsa, D., Serrat, J., López, A.: Video alignment for change detection. IEEE Trans. Image Process. **20**, 1858–1869 (2011)
18. Diego, F., Serrat, J., López, A.: Joint spatio-temporal alignment of sequences. IEEE Trans. Multimedia **15**, 1377–1387 (2013)
19. Ye, G., Liu, Y., Hasler, N., Ji, X.: Performance capture of interacting characters with handheld kinects. In: Proceedings of European Conference on Computer Vision (2012)

Gestalt Principle Based Change Detection and Background Reconstruction

Shi Qiu[1(✉)], Yongsheng Dong[1], Xiaoqiang Lu[1], and Ming Du[2,3]

[1] Center for OPTical IMagery Analysis and Learning (OPTIMAL),
State Key Laboratory of Transient Optics and Photonics, Xi'an Institute of Optics
and Precision Mechanics, Chinese Academy of Sciences, Xi'an, China
qiushi@opt.ac.cn
[2] College of Physics and Information Engineering,
Fuzhou University, Fuzhou, China
[3] Fujian Key Lab of Medical Instrument and Pharmaceutical Technology,
Fuzhou, China

Abstract. Gaussian mixture model based detection algorithms can easily lead to fragmentary due to the fixed number of Gaussian components. In this paper, we propose a gestalt principle based change target extraction method, and further present a background reconstruction algorithm. In particular, firstly we applied the Gaussian mixture model to extract the moving target as others did but this may lead to incomplete extraction. Secondly, we have also tried to apply the frame difference method to extract the moving target more precisely. Finally, we determine to build a static background according to relationships between each frame of a moving target. Experiment results reveal that the proposed detection method outperforms the other three representative detection methods. Moreover, our background reconstruction algorithm is also proved to be very effective and robust in reconstructing the backgrounds of a video.

Keywords: Gestalt visual principle · Moving target extraction · Background reconstruction · Video surveillance

1 Introduction

With the rapid development of video surveillance technology, the computer visual analysis is widely used in video surveillance applications such as object detection and scene understanding [1–3]. Practically, the moving object extraction, background modeling and restoration and the background reconstruction are the key step in the intelligent visual analysis, which is the focus of current research. Conventional algorithms in video can be categorized into three types. The first type is based on pixel [4, 5]. It estimates the moving object's region through build a probability model according to pixel distribution law. But in this case a large number of sample pixels are needed, which means artificial cost is relatively very high. The second type is based on region [6]. It uses the consistency of texture features to reduce influence of the lighting on moving targets and background. But the detection result is not effective when the moving object has small changes only or characteristics are not obvious. The third type

© Springer Nature Singapore Pte Ltd. 2016
Z. Zhang and K. Huang (Eds.): IVS 2016, CCIS 664, pp. 20–29, 2016.
DOI: 10.1007/978-981-10-3476-3_3

is based on the image frames [7, 8]. It detects the moving targets through build an overall mode according to light change principle. But this mode is difficult to build as light changes very quick and itself is very complicate. Whereas all of the above algorithms are based on the computer image calculate level, which cannot meet current needs however. In situation like this, it is difficult to do research on background modeling and moving object extraction currently. To solve the above problems, in this paper we adopt the method of building a Gestalt model based on the principles of Gestalt visual imaging to let computer analyze the video gradually thus to achieve reconstruction of the background and extraction of the moving object, in the purpose of achieving smart surveillance of videos efficiently.

2 Details of Our Algorithm

2.1 Gestalt Psychology

Gestalt theory believes that people can see the objects when interaction happens between the eye and brain. It combines various parts of the visual observations according to certain rules, then making it one unity in an easier to understand [9]. Or else the image will remain disorder or confusion cause it cannot be corrected thereafter.

According to the gestalt vision principle, we detect moving object and reconstruct background as Fig. 1. When we are watching a scene video first, we will concentrate on the region (as block shows in following pic) which we're interested only and ignore the surroundings to simplify the image information. Then we extract target region (dashed line shows in following pic) according to relation between occlusion and moving, to achieve background reconstruction through brain at last, so as to form a stable solid background. Finally reconstruction of the background through the brain to form a stable solid background. That when other follow-up objectives go through this zone, in regardless of how long they have stayed will all be treated as moving targets, does not affect the background image.

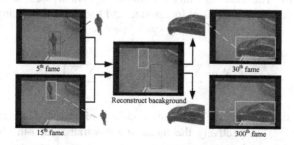

Fig. 1. The visual cognitive processing by gestalt principle

At first we will focus on the moving region roughly, and then construct the model to extract the moving objects accurately. Finally the computer updates the background image and extracts the moving objects by inter-frame information as Fig. 2.

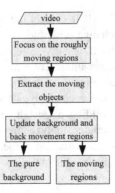

Fig. 2. The algorithm flow chart

2.2 Moving Object Detection

Currently, the main methods of moving object detection include low rank method and optical flow method etc. low rank [4] can extract the moving targets accurately to some degree. But it needs to calculate a large amount of complex data leading it cannot meet video's real-time requirements. Optical flow algorithm [5] computer is very fast, but the model does not consider the feature by target itself. So it does not extract moving objects completely. The above algorithms are based on the image level 'visual cognitive processes. Lead it unable to extract the target and background reconstruction accurately when small amplitude motion or stay there for a long time, also causes impact on understanding, target detection and tracking etc.

Through the study of human cognitive process, when we meet a video scene, we construct background roughly shape through the brain by the video images. Then its attention focuses on the movement region quickly. Finally, computer accurately extracts the motion target by the brain dynamic cognitive process.

According to different image pixel distribution between background and movement, Stauffer and Grimson [10] used the Gaussian mixture model algorithm to simulate pixel values. The Gaussian mixture model algorithm used learning factor to simulate human cognitive process of foreground and background building dynamically by formula (1):

$$P(X_t) = \sum_{i=1}^{k} \omega_{i,t} \times \eta\left(X_t, u_{i,t}, \sum\nolimits_{i,t}\right) \tag{1}$$

Where k is the number of Gaussian model, η represents Gaussian probability density, $\mu_{i,t}$ and $\sum_{i,t}$ respectively the mean and covariance of i-th component. $\omega_{i,t}$ represents the weight of the i-th component of the pixel which updated as formula (2):

$$\omega_{i,t} = (1 - \alpha)\omega_{i,t-1} + \alpha\left(M_{i,t}\right) \tag{2}$$

We priority order the Gaussian distribution model, used front the background model as B which updated as formula (3):

$$B = \arg\min_b \left(\sum_{k=1}^{b} \omega_k > T \right) \tag{3}$$

Where α is the learning factor, $M_{i,t}$ is the matching model. T is a threshold for the minimum ratio from real reaction background of total data A_k is the k-th in the input video frame, $\{Aroi_k\}_N$ represents A_k contain N moving region, $Aroi_k^i$ represents the i-th moving region from A_k. The Gaussian mixture model can extract the moving region roughly. But our analysis by image perspective will miscalculate when the moving target stays a long time or images have small vibration.

Frame difference method used threshold to measure the different value between foreground and background image. Traditional algorithm [11] selects background image is fixed. However, selecting different background images or threshold directly affect the extraction result.

So we improve the Gaussian mixture model and frame difference method to extract the moving targets by properties such as the shape, texture.

Step 1: We convert A_k to grayscale image $Agray_k$ which reduce the amount of calculation.

Step 2: B_k is the k-th background image. It grayscale image is $Bgray_k$ and $B_1 = A_1$.

Step 3: We calculate T_k adaptively as formula (4). where $(x, y) \in Aroi_k$, N_k is the number of pixels from $Aroi_k$.

$$T_k = \begin{cases} \dfrac{\sum\limits_{x,y} |Agray_k(x,y) - Bgray_k(x,y)|}{N_k} & N_k \neq 0 \ (x, y) \in Aroi_k \\ T_{k-1} & N_k = 0 \end{cases} \tag{4}$$

Step 4: Use frame difference method to get target regions as formula (5) and operating morphological as corrosion, expansion to $ID_k(x, y)$, the result regions is $\{Broi_k\}_M$.

$$ID_k(x, y) = \begin{cases} 1 & |Agray_k - Bgray_k| \geq T_k \\ 0 & |Agray_k - Bgray_k| < T_k \end{cases} \tag{5}$$

Step 5: Record the number j compositions series JF, if $Aroi_k^i$ and $Broi_k^j$ ($j = \{1, 2 ..., M\}$) have The public areas.

If $JF \neq \emptyset$ show that the $Aroi_k^i$ is the k-th image moving region, but the small vibration region cannot effectively extract by Gaussian mixture model algorithm, so we used frame difference method to repair region as formula (6):

$$Croi_k^i = \begin{cases} Aroi_k^i |Broi_k^{if_1}|Broi_k^{if_2}...|Broi_k^{if} & jf \in JF, JF \neq \emptyset \\ Aroi_k^i & JF = \emptyset \end{cases} \tag{6}$$

If $JF = \emptyset$ show that the $Aroi_k^i$ is the fore k images moving region, but not sure $Croi_k^i$ is due to annihilation in A_k when the target motion after stay a long time. Or exist in B_k. So we use the canny operator to extract $Agray_k$ and $Bgray_k$ boundary, then contrast the boundary with $Croi_k^i$. If $Agray_k$ is similar $Croi_k^i$ that show $Croi_k^i$ in A_k, we need to extract the target. If $Bgray_k$ is similar $Croi_k^i$ that show $Croi_k^i$ in B_k, we need to update the background. The different brightness between A_k and B_k by $Croi_k^i$ region, that we cannot fusion images simply.

2.3   Background Reconstruction

The computer has been accurately extracting the moving object and this section shows the background reconstruction. Liu *et al.* [12] proposed hierarchical ensemble of background models to reconstruction background. Kim *et al.* [13] structured codebook background mode to fit the distribution characteristics by RGB background pixels. Aqel *et al.* [14] used local adaptive threshold selection method by entropy and generalized Gaussian distribution which can effectively overcome the noises. But those methods just analyze on image perspective, for the target stays a long time and the reconstruction background has ghost regions.

According to the gestalt theory, we analyze cognitive background step by step. We determine the moving target firstly, and then pay attention to the background. Finally we fill the background by the target move. The moving targets are not changed into background and artifacts when they stay a long time or other target across the region. When $Croi_k^i$ in B_k, we need to be updated the B_k by $Croi_k^i$ region. Because the brightness are different between A_k and B_k, If swaps the A_k and B_k by $Croi_k^i$ region. The result image would be uncoordinated. We are defined as

$$T_{k_h} = \frac{\sum_{x,y}(A_{k_h}(x,y) - B_{k_h}(x,y))}{N_k}; \quad (x,y) \in SCroi_k^i - Croi_k^i, h \in H \tag{7}$$

Where H are channels, the RGB image $H = \{1, 2, 3\}$. The Gray image $H = \{1\}$. A_{k_h} and B_{k_h} is the h channel value of A_k and B_k. N_k is the pixel numbers, $Sroi_k^i$ is the minimum rectangle region of $Croi_k^i$. We realize the background update process and achieve the result as formula (8)

$$B_{k_h}(x,y) = A_{k_h}(x,y) - T_{k_h}; \quad (x,y) \in Croi_k^i, h \in H \tag{8}$$

When the background updates, which shows $Croi_k^i$ region has target stay in before k frame. So we need extract moving targets effectively by back movement region. We re-segment the original images $A_l(l < k)$ by the $SCroi_k^i$ region. Extracting the moving region and recasting background image by formula (5), $(x,y) \in (Croi_k^i - Croi_l^i)$.

3   Experimental Results and Analysis

Experiment is used 10 group video database and 5 group video monitoring data. They have three type video data. **Type 1**: At the beginning, there are no target motions, then the target moves. **Type 2**: At the beginning, the target moves, then the target stay there for a long time. **Type 3**: At the beginning, the target is static, then the object moves.

3.1   Detection Performance

Type 1 as Fig. 3(a). We can get the moving targets region roughly by Gaussian mixture model, however the model cannot extract the local little change region as Fig. 3(b) effectively. Then we get the moving targets result as Fig. 3(d) and background result as Fig. 3(e) which integration frame difference method result Fig. 3(c) and (b).

Type 2 as Fig. 4(a). The Gaussian mixture model extract motion regions will be gradually transformed into background as Fig. 4(b) when the targets stay a long time. Frame difference method can restore the motion regions as Fig. 4(c). We gain the moving regions result as Fig. 4(d) by integration Fig. 4(b) and (c).

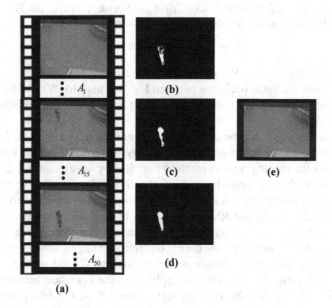

Fig. 3. The moving targets detect result by type 1 (a) input video. (b) $\{Aroi_{50}\}_{10}$, (c) $\{Broi_{50}\}_1$, (d) $\{Croi_{50}\}_1$, (e) B_{50}

The moving regions will be annihilated in the background as Fig. 4(e) and (k) as time goes. Frame difference method can restore the motion regions as Fig. 4(f). But it is not sure the regions from the targets will stay a long time or the region stay in the background image at the beginning. We get the moving regions result as Fig. 4(g) by

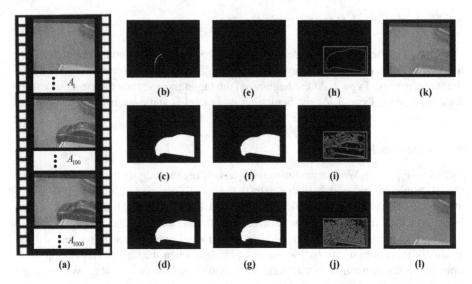

Fig. 4. The moving targets detect result by type 2 (a) input video. (b) $\{Aroi_{100}\}_{12}$, (c) $\{Broi_{100}\}_1$, (d) $\{Croi_{100}\}_1$, (e) $\{Aroi_{1000}\}_0$, (f) $\{Broi_{1000}\}_1$, (g) $\{Croi_{1000}\}_1$, (h) $Croi^1_{1000}$ boundary image, (i) A_{1000} boundary image, (j) B_{1000} boundary image, (k) The background reconstruction by Gaussian mixture model, (l) the update background B_{1000}

integration Fig. 4(e) and (f). We calculate the boundary similarity between Fig. 4(i) and (h), and apply the same operation between Fig. 4(j) and (h). Which shows that the moving region from A_{1000}, the background will not be updated. The result background image is Fig. 4(l).

Type 3 as Fig. 5(a). It produces trailing phenomenon as Fig. 5(b), because the Gaussian mixture model has a gradual process by foreground and background conversion. We get the moving regions result as Fig. 5(d) by integration Fig. 5(b) and (c). Figure 5(d) shows that the target has trailing phenomenon seriously. Figure 5(f) is the result of Gaussian mixture model, and Fig. 5(g) is the result of frame difference method when the target moves. Figure 5(h) is the moving regions result by integration Fig. 5 (g) and (h). We compare Fig. 5(f) and (g), which can suggest the Fig. 5(g) have a separate region. But it cannot be sure the regions from the targets stay a long time or the region stay in the background image at the beginning. We calculate the boundary similarity between Fig. 5(i) and (j), and apply the same operation between Fig. 5(k) and (j), which shows that the moving region from B_{100}, the background will be updated. However, the brightness difference between A_{100} and B_{100}. If they fusion directly, which can non-uniform brightness as Fig. 5(m). Figure 5(n) is the background image by our algorithm.

Experiments show that the algorithm can extract moving object and be reconstructed in complex environment as the moving object stays a long time or images have small vibration.

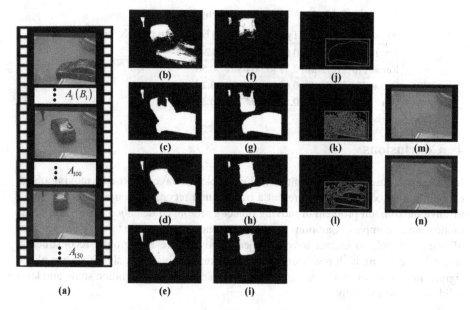

Fig. 5. The moving targets detect result by type 3 (a) input video. (b) $\{Aroi_{100}\}_{13}$, (c) $\{Broi_{100}\}_2$, (d) $\{Croi_{100}\}_2$, (e) 100th frame back movement region, (f) $\{Aroi_{150}\}_{25}$, (g) $\{Broi_{150}\}_3$, (h) $\{Croi_{150}\}_3$, (i) 150th frame back movement region, (j) $Croi^3_{150}$ boundary image, (k) A_{150} boundary image, (l) B_{150} boundary image, (m) The fusion image directly, (n) the update background B_{1000}

3.2 Comparisons with Other Methods

We compare ours and main stream algorithm by segmentation accuracy and processing time. Using the area overlap measure (AOM) as evaluation the segmentation results. It is defined as:

$$\text{AOM}(A, B) = \frac{S(A \cap B)}{S(A \cup B)} \times 100\% \tag{9}$$

Where A is moving region of artificial markers, B is the motion region by algorithm, $S(\cdot)$ is pixel numbers, AOM is the greater and the better. The test results are shown in Table 1.

It is shown that the low rank algorithm based on pixel can extract moving targets, but it needs to calculate all pixels, so the average processing is long when there are no target motions at the beginning, then the target moves. And based on the frame algorithms, we just consider the overall information, processing time is fast, but the accuracy is not that high. We propose the change target extraction and the background reconstruction algorithm based on gestalt principle which the average processing time is shorter than [7], and AOM is lower than [4], but it can be used widely and robustly.

Table 1. AOM and processing time statistics

Algorithm	Type 1	Type 2	Type 3	The average time (S/frame)
Pixel [4]	**0.8501**	0.6430	0.7030	12
Region [6]	0.7800	0.7130	0.6801	0.56
Frame [7]	0.7010	0.6741	0.6423	**0.24**
Our	0.8300	**0.8121**	**0.8012**	0.35

4 Conclusions

In this paper, based on the Gestalt virtual principle we have proposed a moving object extraction method and further present a background reconstruction algorithm in order to solve the difficult problem of moving object's prolonged detention, minor amplitude motion under complex conditions in video sequences. Meanwhile to solve the problem of being not able to extract moving objects and achieve background reconstruction defiantly. Featuring high precision, robust logic and analysis this algorithm can play a significant role in future follow-up video target tracking and recognition study and lay a solid foundation thereby.

References

1. Rav-Acha, A., Pritch, Y., Peleg, S.: Making a long video short: dynamic video synopsis. In: Proceedings of IEEE Conference on Computer Vision and Pattern Recognition, pp. 435–441 (2006)
2. Pritch, Y., Ratovitch, S., Hendel, A., et al.: Clustered synopsis of surveillance video. In: Sixth IEEE International Conference on Advanced Video and Signal Based Surveillance, AVSS 2009, pp. 195–200. IEEE (2009)
3. Feng, S., Lei, Z., Yi, D., et al.: Online content-aware video condensation. In: 2012 IEEE Conference on Computer Vision and Pattern Recognition (CVPR), pp. 2082–2087. IEEE (2012)
4. Shen, X., Wu, Y.: A unified approach to salient object detection via low rank matrix recovery. In: 2012 IEEE Conference on Computer Vision and Pattern Recognition (CVPR), pp. 853–860. IEEE (2012)
5. Yang, L., Cheng, H., Su, J., et al.: Pixel-to-model distance for robust background reconstruction. IEEE Trans. Circ. Syst. Video Technol. 26(5), 903–916 (2016)
6. Satoh, Y., Kaneko, S., Niwa, Y., Yamamoto, K.: Robust object detection using a radial reach filter (RRF). Syst. Comput. Jpn. 35, 63–73 (2004)
7. Patel, C.I., Patel, R.: Illumination invariant moving object detection. Int. J. Comput. Electr. Eng. 5(1), 73–75 (2013)
8. Kumar, N.S., Shobha, G.: Background modeling to detect foreground objects based on ANN and spatio-temporal analysis. Indones. J. Electr. Eng. Comput. Sci. 2(1), 151–160 (2016)
9. Wagemans, J., Feldman, J., Gepshtein, S., et al.: A century of Gestalt psychology in visual perception: II. Conceptual and theoretical foundations. Psychol. Bull. 138(6), 1218 (2012)

10. Stauffer, C., Grimson, W.E.L.: Adaptive background mixture models for real-time tracking. In: IEEE Computer Society Conference on Computer Vision and Pattern Recognition. IEEE (1999)
11. Heikkilä, J., Silvén, O.: A real-time system for monitoring of cyclists and pedestrians. In: Proceedings of the Second IEEE Workshop on Visual Surveillance, pp. 74–81. IEEE, Collins (1999)
12. Liu, N., Wu, H., Lin, L.: Hierarchical ensemble of background models for PTZ-based video surveillance. IEEE Trans. Cybern. **45**(1), 89–102 (2015)
13. Kim, K., Chalidabhongse, T.H., Harwood, D., Davis, L.: Real-time foreground-background segmentation using codebook model. Real-Time Imaging **11**(3), 172–185 (2005)
14. Aqel, S., Aarab, A., Sabri, M.A.: Split procedure combined with entropy for background model. In: 2015 Third World Conference on Complex Systems (WCCS), pp. 1–4. IEEE (2015)

L_0-Regularization Based on Sparse Prior for Image Deblurring

Hongzhang Song$^{(\boxtimes)}$ and Sheng Liu

College of Computer Science and Technology,
Zhejiang University of Technology, Hangzhou, China
songhongzhang4715@126.com, edliu@zjut.edu.cn

Abstract. In this paper we propose a novel L_0 penalty function of both gradient and image itself as the regular term in the total energy function. This regular term is based on sparse prior and solved as part of mathematical optimization problem. Our method not only reserves structure information of the image but also avoids over smooth in the final restoration. We illustrate the applicability and validity of our method through experiments on both synthetic and natural blurry images. Despite we don't have numerous iterations, the convergence rate and result quality outperform the most state-of-the-art methods.

Keywords: Deblurring · Deconvolution · Sparse · Regular term · Norm

1 Introduction

Blind deblurring has been extensively studied in recent years and many significant accomplishments also have been achieved. Due to its non-convex and highly ill-posed property, many natural image priors have made a great contribution to address this kind of problem.

Natural priors focus on the essential features of the sharp image in order to obtain the best model. Cho et al. [1] proposed a computationaly efficient Gaussian prior on the latent image to get the gradient maps for kernel estimation. Shan et al. [2] developed several models together with a new local smoothness prior to approximate the heavy-tailed distribution. Fergus et al. [3] introduced a zero-mean mixture-of-Gaussians to model the gradient magnitudes and adopted a Bayesian approach to find the blur kernel. Nevertheless, none of these models was able to simulate structure information of the sharp image commendably, hence some artifacts appeared in the restored image.

Sparse prior has been emphasized its importance to sharp image and kernel, which hypothesizes that the structure of a sharp image and its corresponding kernel are often sparse. Sparse is usually interpreted as a type of norm, especially L_0 norm, to serve as regular term during the deblurring process. For instance, Krishnan et al. [4] used L_1/L_2 as the regular term, where the L_2 norm in the denominator could be regarded as normalizing the L_1 norm. But it supressed some details of the gradient which could cause bad effects in the result. Xu et al. [5]

© Springer Nature Singapore Pte Ltd. 2016
Z. Zhang and K. Huang (Eds.): IVS 2016, CCIS 664, pp. 30–36, 2016.
DOI: 10.1007/978-981-10-3476-3_4

proposed a piece-wise function to approximate L_0 norm, the obtained image was usually over sparse due to a small threshold. Perrone and Favaro [6] employed Total Variation (similar as L_1 norm) in the optimize process and changed the kernel sparsity into constraints of the total energy function. Yet it had over 1000 iterations with a general result. Likewise, Zuo et al. [7] used a p norm of image gradient, which did not have a better approximation but time consuming.

Based on above discussion and analysis, the main work and contribution of this paper are summarized as follows. (1) We present a novel L_0 norm of both gradient and image itself as the regular term in the optimization formula. The objective of using L_0 norm here is to avoid over smooth and guarantee the sparsity of the result. (2) For the purpose of improving coefficients of the regular terms, we test a range of decimals in several images and select each one with the best performance as our final parameters in the energy function.

We combine a pyramid model with the half-quadratic splitting method [8] to ensure our algorithm converges to a solid solution. Compare with the state-of-the-art methods, we are not only have more similar results under standard quantitative evaluation but also save lots of running time.

2   Algorithm

Generally, image deblurring concentrates on inversing the blurring process and transfers it to a mathematical optimization. The formula we used is formed as,

$$\min_{x,k} \|x \otimes k - y\|^2 + \lambda P(x) + \gamma Q(k), \tag{1}$$

where x and y denote sharp and observed image, respectively. k is the convolved kernel. The first term is data fidelity to reduce the difference between the estimated image after convolving with the kernel and the blurry one. To avoid over fitting, we add two more regular terms $P(x)$ and $Q(k)$.

2.1   New Regular Term

Regular term represented by L_0 norm has been the best reflection of sparse property so far. Due to L_0 norm is highly non-convex, common approach usually creates a function to approximate L_0 norm. Our main work is to build a new loss function which considers both gradient and sharp image. It is formed as follows,

$$P(x) = \theta \|x\|^2 + \varphi(\nabla x), \tag{2}$$

where we use L_2 norm of sharp image to approximate L_0 norm, $\varphi(\nabla x)$ also could be seemed as an approximation of L_0 norm with regard to the gradient. Compare with [5], our approximation maintains some very useful gradients who have small magnitudes and can easily be ignored. The definition of $\varphi(\nabla x)$ is:

$$\varphi(\nabla x) = \begin{cases} \eta \left((\nabla_h x)^2 + (\nabla_v x)^2 \right), & \text{if } (\nabla_h x)^2 + (\nabla_v x)^2 \le \frac{1}{\eta} \\ 1, & \text{otherwise} \end{cases} \tag{3}$$

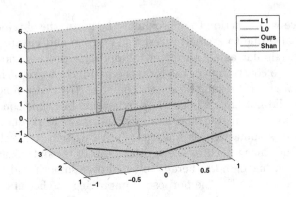

Fig. 1. Plots of our regular term and a few contrasts

where $(\nabla_h x, \nabla_v x)$ separately denote the horizontal and vertical gradients. The main advantage of contrasting to [9] is that we use L_2 instead of L_0 norm on sharp image to avoid over fitting in the results. We show comparison with other sparse-pursuit functions [2,4] in Fig. 1.

The common form of sparse property of blur kernel is: $Q(x) = \|k\|^2$, which is subject to $k \geq 0$ and $\sum k = 1$.

3 Optimization

Our major computation is taken on solving Eq. (1), to do this, a half-quadratic splitting method [8] has been used to divide it into two sub problems Eqs. (4) and (5). We alternately update each one during a few iterations.

$$\min_x \|x \otimes k - y\|^2 + \lambda(\theta \|x\|^2 + \varphi(\nabla x)), \tag{4}$$

$$\min_x \|x \otimes k - y\|^2 + \gamma \|k\|^2. \tag{5}$$

3.1 Compute x

Consider $\varphi(\nabla x)$ is a piece-wise function which would make Eq. (4) highly non-convex. We introduce an auxiliary vector (h, v) which is corresponding to $(\nabla_h x, \nabla_v x)$, then we rewrite Eq. (3) as

$$\varphi(\nabla x) = \eta((\nabla_h x - h)^2 + (\nabla_v x - v)^2) + M(|h|^0 + |v|^0), \tag{6}$$

where M is a binary mask function satisfies $M(|h|^0 + |v|^0) = 0$ only if $h = 0, v = 0$ and 1 otherwise. η has to be large enough to make sure auxiliary vector work.

$$(h, v) = \begin{cases} (0, 0), & \text{if } (\nabla_h x)^2 + (\nabla_v x)^2 \leq \frac{1}{\eta} \\ (\nabla_h x, \nabla_v x), & \text{otherwise} \end{cases} \tag{7}$$

Similar to [5], Eq. (7) serves as the solution of Eq. (6), which means it also satisfies minimizing Eq. (3).

After fixing (h, v), we can update x by substitute Eq. (6) into Eq. (4), then derive it in the frequency domain and yield its optimum solution,

$$x = \mathcal{F}^{-1} \left(\frac{\overline{\mathcal{F}(k)} \times \mathcal{F}(y) + \lambda\eta(\overline{\mathcal{F}(\nabla_h)} \times \mathcal{F}(h) + \overline{\mathcal{F}(\nabla_v)} \times \mathcal{F}(v))}{\overline{\mathcal{F}(k)} \times \mathcal{F}(k) + \lambda\theta + \lambda\eta(\overline{\mathcal{F}(\nabla_h)} \times \mathcal{F}(\nabla_h) + \overline{\mathcal{F}(\nabla_v)} \times \mathcal{F}(\nabla_v))} \right),$$
(8)

where $\mathcal{F}(\cdot)$ is the FFT operator and $\mathcal{F}^{-1}(\cdot)$ denotes the inverse FFT. $\overline{\mathcal{F}(\cdot)}$ means the complex conjugate. Both multiplication and division operate on element wise.

3.2 Compute k

Directly optimize Eq. (5) has been proved that it will lead to an inaccurate solution [1]. We use $\nabla_* x$ and $\nabla_* y$ instead of x and y, then define $S(k)$ as

$$S(k) = \|\nabla_h x \otimes k - \nabla_h y\|^2 + \|\nabla_h x \otimes k - \nabla_h y\|^2 + \gamma \|k\|^2.$$
(9)

Here a conjugate gradient method is employed to minimize $S(k)$.

We show the comparison of our estimated kernel with a few others and the kernel similarity [10] from dataset [11] during each iterations in Fig. 2.

Algorithm 1. Overview of Deblurring

Input: Observed image y
Output: Sharp image x and blur kernel k
1: **for** $i = 1 : 5$ **do**
2:     update (h, v) using Eq. (7).
3:     update x using Eq. (8).
4:     update k using Eq.•(9).
5: **end for**
6: non-blind deconvolution.

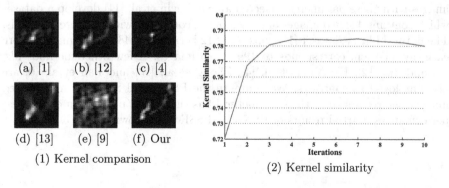

(1) Kernel comparison   (2) Kernel similarity

Fig. 2. Convergence of the proposed algorithm

3.3   Non-blind Deconvolution

The intermediate sharp image x from Sect. 3.1 has not yet qualified as final output. After fixing kernel in Sect. 3.2, we use k as input of a non-blind deconvolution method to estimate the final sharp image. Here we adopt Krishnan's method [14] which is based on Hyper-Laplacian prior to gain the first sharp image. Then similar as [9], we use Eq. (8) to solve a second image, together combine with a bilateral filtering mask to obtain the final version. Experiments show that such method would suppress the artifacts in the estimated images.

4   Experiments

In this section, we first explain how we determine the values of coefficient λ, θ, γ. Take λ as an example, we test our method on several different images in the range of $3e - 4$ to $2e - 2$ and leave others intact. After that we count the quantitative evaluation of each value on each image and select the highest as the final λ. As for η, we initialize it with $\lambda/2$ and increase it during each iteration.

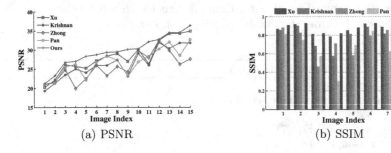

(a) PSNR   (b) SSIM

Fig. 3. PSNR and SSIM quantitative evaluation on [11] and [15]

Afterwords, we employ our method on both synthetic and natural blurry images with these parameters selected above. Levin et al. [11] develop a dataset which contains 4 sharp images and each one is convolved with 8 different kernels. The natural blurry dataset [15] consists of 12 kernels and 48 blurry images where each one of them corresponds to 199 sharp images. A few other methods like Xu and Jia [12], Krishnan et al. [4], Zhong et al. [13] and Pan et al. [9] are also employed as contrasts. We compute the PSNR and SSIM on all restored images, the results show that our method has the largest proportion of the best performances. Partial results of PSNR and SSIM are shown in Fig. 3.

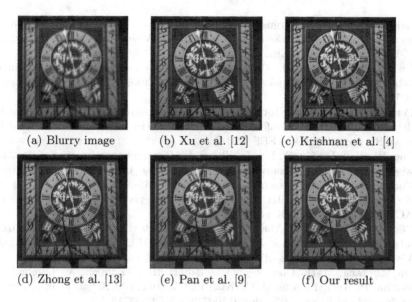

(a) Blurry image   (b) Xu et al. [12]   (c) Krishnan et al. [4]

(d) Zhong et al. [13]   (e) Pan et al. [9]   (f) Our result

Fig. 4. Examples of natural images with kernel size of 41×41 from dataset [14]

5 Discussion

Many deblurring methods are based on the sparse prior, that is using a formula similar to Eq. (1) to transform deblurring to a mathematical optimization problem. The regular term has multiple modalities and is the main difference among these methods, but all of them could be seemed as some kind of approximations of L_0 norm. The proposed method is not only constrain the gradient of sharp image by using L_0 norm, but also add constraints on sharp image itself. Compared with existing algorithms, we have decreased the smoothing constraints on the final estimated image and meantime increased the convergence speed.

Acknowledgements. The work described in this paper was supported by Zhejiang Provincial Natural Science Foundation of China under Grant number LY15F020031 and LQ16F030007, National Natural Science Foundation of China (NSFC) under Grant numbers 11302195 and 61401397.

References

1. Cho, S., Lee, S.: Fast motion deblurring. ACM Trans. Graph. (TOG) **28**, 145 (2009). ACM
2. Shan, Q., Jia, J., Agarwala, A.: High-quality motion deblurring from a single image. ACM Trans. Graph. (TOG) **27**, 73 (2008). ACM
3. Fergus, R., Singh, B., Hertzmann, A., Roweis, S.T., Freeman, W.T.: Removing camera shake from a single photograph. ACM Trans. Graph. (TOG) **25**, 787–794 (2006). ACM

4. Krishnan, D., Tay, T., Fergus, R.: Blind deconvolution using a normalized sparsity measure. In: 2011 IEEE Conference on Computer Vision and Pattern Recognition (CVPR), pp. 233–240. IEEE (2011)
5. Xu, L., Zheng, S., Jia, J.: Unnatural l0 sparse representation for natural image deblurring. In: IEEE Conference on Computer Vision and Pattern Recognition (CVPR) (2013)
6. Perrone, D., Favaro, P.: Total variation blind deconvolution: the devil is in the details. In: 2014 IEEE Conference on Computer Vision and Pattern Recognition (CVPR), pp. 2909–2916. IEEE (2014)
7. Zuo, W., Ren, D., Gu, S., Lin, L., Zhang, L.: Discriminative learning of iteration-wise priors for blind deconvolution. In: Proceedings of the IEEE Conference on Computer Vision and Pattern Recognition, pp. 3232–3240 (2015)
8. Xu, L., Lu, C., Xu, Y., Jia, J.: Image smoothing via L_0 gradient minimization. ACM Trans. Graph. (TOG) **30**, 174 (2011). ACM
9. Pan, J., Hu, Z., Su, Z., Yang, M.H.: Deblurring text images via L_0-regularized intensity and gradient prior. In: Proceedings of the IEEE Conference on Computer Vision and Pattern Recognition (2014)
10. Hu, Z., Yang, M.-H.: Good regions to deblur. In: Fitzgibbon, A., Lazebnik, S., Perona, P., Sato, Y., Schmid, C. (eds.) ECCV 2012. LNCS, vol. 7576, pp. 59–72. Springer, Heidelberg (2012). doi:10.1007/978-3-642-33715-4_5
11. Levin, A., Weiss, Y., Durand, F., Freeman, W.T.: Understanding and evaluating blind deconvolution algorithms. In: 2009 IEEE Conference on Computer Vision and Pattern Recognition, CVPR 2009, pp. 1964–1971. IEEE (2009)
12. Xu, L., Jia, J.: Two-phase kernel estimation for robust motion deblurring. In: Daniilidis, K., Maragos, P., Paragios, N. (eds.) ECCV 2010. LNCS, vol. 6311, pp. 157–170. Springer, Heidelberg (2010). doi:10.1007/978-3-642-15549-9_12
13. Zhong, L., Cho, S., Metaxas, D., Paris, S., Wang, J.: Handling noise in single image deblurring using directional filters. In: Proceedings of the IEEE Conference on Computer Vision and Pattern Recognition, pp. 612–619 (2013)
14. Krishnan, D., Fergus, R.: Fast image deconvolution using hyper-laplacian priors. In: Advances in Neural Information Processing Systems, pp. 1033–1041 (2009)
15. Köhler, R., Hirsch, M., Mohler, B., Schölkopf, B., Harmeling, S.: Recording and playback of camera shake: benchmarking blind deconvolution with a real-world database. In: Fitzgibbon, A., Lazebnik, S., Perona, P., Sato, Y., Schmid, C. (eds.) ECCV 2012. LNCS, vol. 7578, pp. 27–40. Springer, Heidelberg (2012). doi:10.1007/978-3-642-33786-4_3

A Large-Scale Distributed Video Parsing and Evaluation Platform

Kai Yu[(✉)], Yang Zhou, Da Li, Zhang Zhang, and Kaiqi Huang

Center for Research on Intelligent Perception and Computing,
Institute of Automation, Chinese Academy of Sciences, Beijing, China
kyu_115s@hotmail.com

Abstract. Visual surveillance systems have become one of the largest data sources of Big Visual Data in real world. However, existing systems for video analysis still lack the ability to handle the problems of scalability, expansibility and error-prone, though great advances have been achieved in a number of visual recognition tasks and surveillance applications, e.g., pedestrian/vehicle detection, people/vehicle counting. Moreover, few algorithms explore the specific values/characteristics in large-scale surveillance videos. To address these problems in large-scale video analysis, we develop a scalable video parsing and evaluation platform through combining some advanced techniques for Big Data processing, including Spark Streaming, Kafka and Hadoop Distributed Filesystem (HDFS). Also, a Web User Interface is designed in the system, to collect users' degrees of satisfaction on the recognition tasks so as to evaluate the performance of the whole system. Furthermore, the highly extensible platform running on the long-term surveillance videos makes it possible to develop more intelligent incremental algorithms to enhance the performance of various visual recognition tasks.

1 Introduction

Intelligent visual surveillance (IVS) has long been one of the most important applications of computer vision technologies. Intelligent surveillance video analysis is a demand-increasing research topic along with the raising of consciousness of public security and explosive increase of deployment of surveillance devices. In the past decades, most researchers aimed to solve separate visual tasks, e.g., background modeling [1–3], object detection [4–6], motion tracking [7,8], person re-identification [9,10] and attribute recognition [11,12], which is because early researchers [13] considered the complexity of whole surveillance task, thus divided the whole system into several separate steps with a divide-and-conquer strategy. And one ordinary IVS system is simple a fixed execution flow of these sub-tasks. However, the era of Big Data raises new challenges for IVS systems. First, to explore values in large-scale visual surveillance video, it is urged to solve the problem of scalability and error-prone of large-scale video data processing. Second, to discover correlations in various visual information, it need solve the problem of expansibility and flexibility of deploying new visual analysis modules. Third, the system could be improved adaptively and incrementally in its

Z. Zhang and K. Huang (Eds.): IVS 2016, CCIS 664, pp. 37–43, 2016.
DOI: 10.1007/978-981-10-3476-3_5

running lifetime, thus the users's feedbacks should be collected to optimize the models for different visual tasks. Unfortunately, in previous work, few efforts were devoted to these problems.

In this work, to address these problems, we present a novel Large-scale Video Parsing and Evaluation Platform (LaS-VPE Platform) based on some advanced techniques for Big Data processing, including Spark Streaming, Kafka and HDFS [14]. This platform can run easily and flexibly on distributed clusters, making full use of large-scale computation resources. High-level abstraction of vision tasks and usage of Spark Streaming and Kafka make it possible to add or replace any algorithm modules at any time and robust to faults, thus easy to maintain and computation-resources-saving. The high flexibility of the system also enables users to specify their own execution plan. Also the well-designed platform and Web UI make it easy for both developers to extend the system and users to operate on the system.

The main contributions of this paper are listed below:

1. We propose a detailed and integrated solution for surveillance scene parsing and performance evaluation with large-scale video data.
2. We solve some technical issues in adopting and integrating Spark Streaming and Kafka in large-scale video processing.
3. The implementation of this platform is an open-source project, and we will share it in GitHub, so anyone can make use of it while referring to this paper.

2   Relating Works

There has been researches on IVS systems which show some common interests with our work. The VisFlow [15] system also combines machine vision with big data analysis, featuring high accuracy and efficiency. It can compute execution plans for different vision queries, by building a relational dataflow system. Compared to this work, the LaS-VPE platform does not provide optimization for execution plan, but instead enables users to easily create their own plans with Web UI. Parameters and execution order can be specified in any valid form on every query, making it highly customizable. The optimization work is left to users or done by future extern modules.

Qi et al. proposed the Visual Turing Test system [16] for deep understanding in long-term and multi-camera captured videos. It presents a well-designed system for video-evaluation utilizing scene-centered representation and story-line based queries. However, this work does not focus on system efficiency. Our system emphasizes less on visual algorithm evaluation concepts, but spend more effort on improving the feasibility of evaluation on massive video data by distributed computing techniques and flexible system design.

3   Platform Design

In this section, we describe the design of our LaS-VPE platform. The platform is powered by Spark Streaming on YARN and Kafka. For better understanding of the mechanism of this platform, readers are recommended to first read through some introductions and have a rough understanding of mechanisms and terms of Spark Streaming and Kafka.

3.1   Platform Framework

The LaS-VPE platform is divided into several modules. Each module is responsible for one kind of system affairs, like meta-data saving, extern message handling, and execution of different versions of different visual recognition algorithms. Each module runs permanently, unless the administrator manually terminates it. Communication among different modules is powered by Kafka, which is a high-throughput, distributed, publish-subscribe messaging system.

The LaS-VPE platform also possesses a Web UI. Users can create a certain task in it, and command the tasks to flow through the modules in a specified graph. A task thus has specified input and execution route, and can end with several outputs, including saving meta-data to databases or hard disks and responding user queries in the Web UI.

3.2   Task Flow and Communication

To address the problem in traditional IVS systems that only a few preset execution plans are available and to enhance the expansibility and flexibility of the system, we enable our modules to be executed in user-defined plans. Each execution corresponding to a vision query is called a task. Each task can specify the order of visual recognition sub-modules in a form of flow graph of modules. For simplicity, a flow graph must be directed acyclic. One module may exist more than once in a flow graph, if it needs to be executed more than once, enabling finite execution circles to be dissembled and operated in one task.

Tasks pass among modules as a flow of Kafka messages. A Kafka message contains a key field and a value field. The key field records a Universal Unique Identifier (UUID) assigned to each task, which is generated along with the task generation in the Web UI. The value field records a serialized byte array of a special class TaskData, which is illustrated in Fig. 1. It contains three fields: result data from the sender module, identifier of next module to execute (NME) and the flow graph structure of the task. A flow graph structure is then described by two parts: nodes and links, where each node specifies a module to be executed as well as some parameters and extra data for that single execution. Each directed link indicates that after the execution of the module specified by the head node, its results should be sent to the module specified by the tail node, and that module shall be executed some time afterwards.

Since the graph is a directed acyclic graph, it is able to be topological-sorted. Each time a module receives a message, the NME corresponds to the module itself, so the module can find itself in the graph according to this field. If the module takes more than one input node and some inputs currently have not arrived yet, the module cannot be immediately executed, and the current message sent to this module will be cached temporarily. Multiple pieces of cached messages

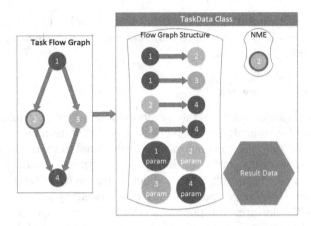

Fig. 1. This picture illustrates how to represent a logical task flow graph in a TaskData class. The flow graph structure is an adjacency list of the graph. The NME field specified the next module to execute. In this picture, this module corresponds to the node numbered 2. The result data field's content is not considered here. It will be analyzed by the consuming part of the module.

will be merged and accumulated in the module. When the input requirement is satisfied, the module starts an execution with the accumulated data.

3.3   Kafka-Based Inter-module Communication

We use Kafka for communication between modules, so as to decouple the system and enhance the flexibility and extensibility of the system. By doing so, modules need not be written and compiled together and thus become isolated. When one module dies due to some exception or deliberate termination, it does not affect the others, and the input data to this module will be cached by the Kafka, so when this module recovers or is replaced by a new version of it, these input data can be correctly consumed and processed. Also, the destinations of output can be specified by the task flow graph described above, so it need not modify and recompile a module if we want it to output to some alternative destinations.

Kafka topics can be divided into groups for different type of messages, such as topics for pedestrian tracks and topics for pedestrian attributes. However, topics are not shared among different vision modules. Each module owns one or more topics corresponding to its input data types. For example, if Module $M1$ and $M2$ both take in pedestrian attributes and tracks as input, $M1$ owns two topics named $M1$-$Pedestrian$-$Attribute$ and $M1$-$Pedestrian$-$Track$ respectively, while $M2$ owns another two topics named $M2$-$Pedestrian$-$Attribute$ and $M2$-$Pedestrian$-$Track$ respectively. If some modules have produced some attributes and is commanded to send to both $M1$ and $M2$, the Kafka producers inside these modules need to send the attributes to both $M1$-$Pedestrian$-$Attribute$ and $M2$-$Pedestrian$-$Attribute$ message queues. In this way, the task flow graph actually does not specifies which module to output to, but instead which topic to output to, since a topic belongs to exactly one module.

3.4   Spark Streaming and YARN

For large-scale video data processing, clusters are preferred for high through-out computation. We choose Spark Streaming to enable distributed computation since it guarantees realtime processing, and use YARN to manage the cluster. We view each module as a Spark Streaming application. Applications are submitted to YARN by the SparkLauncher class programmatically, then run permanently. Multiple applications may run simultaneously and independently on YARN. It is easy to terminate applications using the Web UI of YARN. This means we can choose only part of the modules in the platform to run, and terminate any of them whenever we want, thus saving computation resources.

In the LaS-VPE platform, a streaming context usually consists of three stages: Kafka message receiving stage, message re-organizing stage (optional) and message processing stage. The Kafka message receiving stage receive messages from Kafka then transfers them into Discretized Streams (DStreams), which abstractly represents a continuous stream of data. In each call of the final message processing stage, a certain extern algorithm, such as a tracking algorithm, is run simultaneously on multiple workers to process the data delivered to them. The results are then output in various forms, like using a KafkaProducer class to send it to Kafka, or using a FileSystem class to send it to HDFS, etc.

3.5   Web UI Design and Evaluation

The LaS-VPE platform provides a Web UI for generating tasks, monitoring the applications in the platform, and querying the visual recognition results. The task generating UI allows users to easily create a flow graph of jobs within each task. The UI server is responsible to transform the graph into the data form mentioned above and send it to the processing modules, then listen to execution results.

The web page for querying results does not directly communicate with the processing modules. Since we force each processing module to save their meta-data and results on HDFS or databases, the query-solving server seeks results at these locations. This makes results endurable and easy to access outside the processing cluster. Also, a feedback field is provided in the result displaying pages, varying according to the type of results, to allow users to simply mark their satisfaction of the results or provide detailed revision on the results they see. For example, in Re-ID applications, results are displayed in a form of ranked candidate photos that are predicted to be the most similar to the target, so users can give feedback by simply selecting the ground-truth ones, and satisfaction as well as supervision information can be both inferred. These feedbacks are stored into a database and can be used for future semi-supervised or supervised incremental training of all the algorithms used for the tasks.

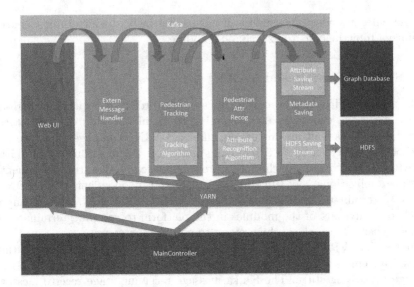

Fig. 2. This picture shows a sample framework. Modules are submitted to YARN, and task flows start from extern web UI. Results are saved in the meta-data saving module.

Combining these features, one can specify various combinations of algorithms and configurations of each vision algorithm modules, then evaluate them on any database representing a particular application scene, so it is easy and low-costing to find out the best settings for any new applications scenes, thus exploiting the ability of video parsing algorithms in maximum extent. The whole system is illustrated in Fig. 2.

4   Conclusions

In this paper, we proposed a novel Video Parsing and Evaluation Platform to solve problems existing in ordinary video surveillance systems like low flexibility and extensibility and lack of user feedback collecting functions. The VPE-Platform can run robustly on distributed clusters, support highly customized job flow and easy maintaining, and collect user feedback for incremental training. Some experiments will be added in the future to show the design validity and high performance of the platform.

Acknowledgements. This work was supported by the National Natural Science Foundation of China under Grants 61473290, the National High Technology Research and Development Program of China (863 Program) under Grant 2015AA042307, and the international partnership program of Chinese Academy of Sciences, grant No. 173211KYSB20160008.

References

1. François, A.R., Medioni, G.G.: Adaptive color background modeling for real-time segmentation of video streams. In: Proceedings of the International Conference on Imaging Science, Systems, and Technology, vol. 1, pp. 227–232 (1999)
2. Rodriguez, P., Wohlberg, B.: Incremental principal component pursuit for video background modeling. J. Math. Imaging Vis. **55**, 1–18 (2016)
3. Zhang, X., Huang, T., Tian, Y., Gao, W.: Background-modeling-based adaptive prediction for surveillance video coding. IEEE Trans. Image Process. **23**, 769–784 (2014)
4. Nadimi, S., Bhanu, B.: Physical models for moving shadow and object detection in video. IEEE Trans. Pattern Anal. Mach. Intell. **26**, 1079–1087 (2004)
5. Tripathi, S., Lipton, Z.C., Belongie, S., Nguyen, T.: Context matters: refining object detection in video with recurrent neural networks. arXiv preprint arXiv:1607.04648 (2016)
6. Oreifej, O., Li, X., Shah, M.: Simultaneous video stabilization and moving object detection in turbulence. IEEE Trans. Pattern Anal. Mach. Intell. **35**, 450–462 (2013)
7. Xu, J.B., Po, L.M., Cheung, C.K.: Adaptive motion tracking block matching algorithms for video coding. IEEE Trans. Circuits Syst. Video Technol. **9**, 1025–1029 (1999)
8. Foxlin, E., Wormell, D., Browne, T.C., Donfrancesco, M.: Motion tracking system and method using camera and non-camera sensors. US Patent 8,696,458 (2014)
9. Hamdoun, O., Moutarde, F., Stanciulescu, B., Steux, B.: Person re-identification in multi-camera system by signature based on interest point descriptors collected on short video sequences. In: Second ACM/IEEE International Conference on Distributed Smart Cameras, ICDSC 2008, pp. 1–6. IEEE (2008)
10. Wang, T., Gong, S., Zhu, X., Wang, S.: Person re-identification by discriminative selection in video ranking. arXiv:1601.06260v1 [cs.CV] (2016)
11. Fukui, H., Yamashita, T., Yamauchi, Y., Fujiyoshi, H., Murase, H.: Robust pedestrian attribute recognition for an unbalanced dataset using mini-batch training with rarity rate. In: 2016 IEEE Intelligent Vehicles Symposium (IV), pp. 322–327. IEEE (2016)
12. Deng, Y., Luo, P., Loy, C.C., Tang, X.: Pedestrian attribute recognition at far distance. In: Proceedings of the 22nd ACM International Conference on Multimedia, pp. 789–792. ACM (2014)
13. Wang, L., Hu, W., Tan, T.: Recent developments in human motion analysis. Pattern Recogn. **36**, 585–601 (2003)
14. Shvachko, K., Kuang, H., Radia, S., Chansler, R.: The hadoop distributed file system. In: 2010 IEEE 26th Symposium on Mass Storage Systems and Technologies (MSST), pp. 1–10. IEEE (2010)
15. Lu, Y., Chowdhery, A., Kandula, S.: Visflow: a relational platform for efficient large-scale video analytics. In: BigVision (2016)
16. Qi, H., Wu, T., Lee, M.W., Zhu, S.C.: A restricted visual turing test for deep scene and event understanding. arXiv preprint arXiv:1512.01715 (2015)

Tracking, Robotics

Autonomous Wheeled Robot Navigation with Uncalibrated Spherical Images

Lingyan Ran[✉], Yanning Zhang, Tao Yang, and Peng Zhang

School of Computer Science and Engineering,
Northwestern Polytechnical University, Xi'an, Shaanxi, China
Lingyanran@gmail.com

Abstract. This paper focuses on the use of spherical cameras for autonomous robot navigation tasks. Previous works of literature mainly lie in two categories: scene oriented simultaneous localization and mapping and robot oriented heading fields lane detection and trajectory tracking. Those methods face the challenges of either high computation cost or heavy labelling and calibration requirements. In this paper, we propose to formulate the spherical image navigation as an image classification problem, which significantly simplifies the orientation estimation and path prediction procedure and accelerates the navigation process. More specifically, we train an end-to-end convolutional network on our spherical image dataset with novel orientation categories labels. This trained network can give precise predictions on potential path directions with single spherical images. Experimental results on our Spherical-Navi dataset demonstrate that the proposed approach outperforms the comparing methods in realistic applications.

1 Introduction

In the field of autonomous driving, vision-based navigation research has long been a hot topic. On various platforms, like quadrotors, self-driving cars, and robotics, multiple types of sensors and cameras have been facilitated to improve the machine intelligence. In this paper, we propose an alternative approach of using a convolutional neural network (CNN) for addressing the problem of autonomous robot navigation with spherical cameras. Details of our device and framework are shown in Fig. 1.

Accurate position and orientation estimation of a camera is one of the most important tasks for robotic navigation problems. In most scenarios, simultaneously building up the 3D maps of the world while tracking the location and the orientation of the camera is a common approach for a navigation task. In the last two decades, simultaneous localization and mapping (SLAM) method and various derivatives have been dominating this topic. Various systems have been proposed, for example, PTAM [1] etc. Recently, Caruso et al. [2] successfully accomplish a SLAM system for direct use of omnidirectional cameras.

All the SLAM based systems have achieved great performance and offer users a set of candidate solutions for navigation tasks. However, when it comes to

Z. Zhang and K. Huang (Eds.): IVS 2016, CCIS 664, pp. 47–55, 2016.
DOI: 10.1007/978-981-10-3476-3_6

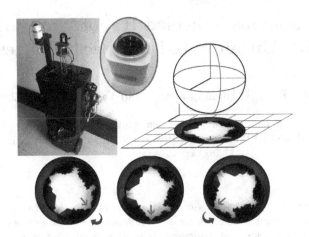

Fig. 1. A spherical driving robot. For spherical images, the central bottom pixels are the front heading of a robot and the red arrows points to the potential path. Our motivation is to generate navigation signals with the severely distorted spherical images. (Color figure online)

moving platforms, like tablet PCs, quadrotors, and moving robotics as in our case, limited computational capabilities pushes the SLAM based navigation task a higher complexity level. Therefore, seeking a low-cost solution is important.

Inspired by the human vision system, another group of methods focus on the problem of road detection and trajectory planning. An intelligent robot could follow the visual paths via local road segmentation [3] and trajectory prediction [4]. For example, Lu et al. [5] build up a hierarchical vision sensor based method for robust road detection in challenging road scenes. Chang et al. [6] present a vision-based navigation and localization system using two biologically-inspired scene understanding models which are studied from human visual capabilities.

In spite of their simplicity, human vision inspired methods highly rely on local features for segmentation tasks and usually lose a whole sense of the environment. What's more, for spherical images, the calibration and wrapping process further complicates those solutions.

As early in the 90s, Pomerleau [7] has treated the road following task as a classification problem. Later on, Hadsell et al. [8] develop a similar system for navigation in unknown environments. Recently, Giusti et al. [9] define the camera orientation estimation as a three-class classification problem (Left, Front, Right) and capture a set of forest trail images with 3 head-mounted cameras, each pointing to one direction. Given one frame image, their trained model can tell a robot whether it need to make a left/right turn or keep straight forward. One drawback here is that the fixed cameras are not flexible for tasks with higher orientation precision demands. For more turning control signals, more cameras are needed. This may not be a good solution for complex applications.

Inspired by [7], in this paper, we propose to make navigation predictions by classifying spherical images into different rotation categories. One characteristic of spherical images is that it captures a wide view of 360° natural scenes and thus gives much more potentially useful information than those plane images. For generating training images of different orientations, we could just make a rotation of the original front viewed images and do not need to recapture the scene. The contributions of our paper are as following:

- We formulate this spherical camera navigation task as an image classification problem and design an end-to-end CNN for it. It's efficient for reality applications, where we don't need to do pixel-wise labelling of roads or build a complex 3D world with unreasonable high computation and memory costs.
- We build one spherical navigation dataset and raise a novel labelling strategy, which enables us to generate various training images for different complexity and precision applications with a minor change in the labelling process.

2   Navigation Network

Deep convolutional networks have been widely used in many computer vision tasks, e.g. image recognition [10], image segmentation [11], object detection [12] etc. In this paper, we train a convolutional network to estimate accurate robot heading pose orientation in the navigation task using raw spherical images. Details on the problem formulation and the network design are in the following.

2.1   Navigation via Classification Formulation

Accurate position and orientation estimation of a robot is a basic step for building navigation systems. Other than doing high computation cost processes like SLAM or lane segmentation, a novel approach of formulating navigation as an image classification problem is described in details in this subsection.

Figure 1 illustrates a general view of our capturing platform. An upward-looking spherical camera is fixed on top of a wheeled robot, which can capture images with detailed information of its 360° surroundings. Considering when the robot is wandering around within a campus, our problem is to tell the robot to turn left/right or keep straight forward with spherical frames in real-time.

Given a set of N spherical images $X \in \mathbb{R}^D$, we want to get the potential navigation direction $y \in Y$, with a range of $[-k, +k]$, where k equals to $1, 2, 3, \ldots$ for different complexities. Let $y = 0$ denote going straight forward, $y < 0$ for turning left, and $y > 0$ for turning right. For learning the model, the goal is to minimize the global prediction error of: $L = \sum_{n=1}^{N}[1 - \delta(\hat{y}_n, y_n)]$, in which $\hat{y}_n = F(x_n)$ is our prediction for sample (x_n, y_n), $\delta(a, b)$ equals to one if $a = b$ and zero otherwise. The nonlinear warping model $F(x; w, b)$ will be learned next.

2.2   Network Structure

Inspired by the extraordinary works of Alexnet [10] and its extension Giusti et al. [9], we adopt a similar CNN for the spherical image classification problem.

Table 1. The network structure and layer setups of CNN used in our experiments.

	Features	[9]	Model 1	Model 2
0	$3 \times 101 \times 101$	Inputs	Inputs	Inputs
1	$32 \times 98 \times 98$	Conv	Conv	Conv
2	$32 \times 49 \times 49$	Pool	Pool	Pool
3	-	Tanh	P/ReLU	BN+PReLU
4	$32 \times 46 \times 46$	Conv	Conv	Conv
5	$32 \times 23 \times 23$	Pool	Pool	Pool
6	-	Tanh	P/ReLU	BN+PReLU
7	$32 \times 20 \times 20$	Conv	Conv	Conv
8	$32 \times 10 \times 10$	Pool	Pool	Pool
9	-	Tanh	P/ReLU	BN+PReLU
10	$32 \times 7 \times 7$	Conv	Conv	Conv
11	$32 \times 3 \times 3$	Pool	Pool	Pool
12	-	Tanh	P/ReLU	BN+PReLU
13	288–200	FC1	FC1	FC1
14	-	Tanh	P/ReLU	PReLU
15	200–K	FC2	FC2	FC2

A convolutional network conventionally consists of several successive pairs of convolutional layers (Conv), pooling layers (Pool) and fully connected layers (FC). Our network consists of four Conv layers and two FC layers. Each Conv layer is followed by a max-pooling layer to enhance the local contrast.

Table 1 presents the detailed layer-wise network setups. Since Giusti et al. [9] choose to use the scaled hyperbolic tangent activation function (Tanh) and do not give much analysis on the non-linear warping functions, we first put some effort on that. We find out that both Rectified Linear Units (ReLU) [13] and Parametric Rectified Linear Units (PReLU) [14] outperform Tanh units. Here we choose the better one (PReLU in model 1, Table 1) for later experiments.

Optimizing a deep neural network may not be easy because of the gradient vanishing/exploding trouble, and it is highly likely that our model may get stuck in a saddle point and could not well tune the lower level features. This is especially serious for spherical images, as most of them are similar in appearance and the gradient may not be of much different. We here adopt the Batch Normalization (BN) [15] method in model 2, Table 1, which forces the network activations to vary across examples. In this way, we could not only accelerate the training of networks but also achieve a better classification performance.

During training, the networks are optimized with the adagrad strategy, which relieves us from trying learning rates and momentum hyper-parameters back and forth. Further details and analysis on the performance of the network configurations are given in the experiment section.

3 Spherical-Navi Dataset

To train a model that could accurately classify images, a dataset with balanced class distribution is required. Since a spherical image has the characteristic that the orientation change of camera viewing only results in a rotation of the spherical images, we could generate simulation images with various robot orientations from one single image. In this way, the drawback of [9] being not flexible is not a serious problem anymore.

Data Capturing. In total, ten video sequences are captured using a spherical camera when the robot is wandering around within a campus. Each video is captured at 60 frames per second with a high resolution of 4608×3456 pixels. To ensure that neural networks actually model the whole dataset well instead of just memorizing the scene, we carefully design the navigation path so that there are fewer overlaps among those video clips.

Data Labelling. For a navigation task with K turning control signals, we actually can generate any orientation posed image by a specific rotation of the original one. For stability, when generating images for different classes, a larger field is given to front views. That's because, in this way, the robot has a higher probability of keeping on going straight other than frequent left/right turn interruptions. Figure 2 gives an illustration of how the image of different classes look like on one same street corner with $K = 7$. Here, we have those random rotations of $(-30°, +30°)$ as front view (i.e. k = 0) and the rest regions are equally divided into six orientation fields.

Data Argumentation. Due to the robot moving jitter, some frames may not contain satisfying high-quality contents. Without loss of generality, in this paper, video sequences are resampled at two frames per second. In total, there are 8000 images for training and 6000 images for testing.

Before feeding into the network, we also apply some pre-processes on the spherical images. Since the spherical camera is fixed upward looking, it captures much unnecessary information to the prediction, such as the central sky pixels in Fig. 2. In the training procedure, those central pixels are masked out. In our experiment, we get about 1% improvement on average when the central pixels are masked out. All images are then normalized in the YUV space with zero-mean and unit variance to reduce the lighting changing effects.

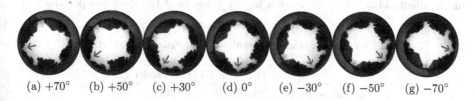

(a) +70°   (b) +50°   (c) +30°   (d) 0°   (e) −30°   (f) −50°   (g) −70°

Fig. 2. Sample images from 7-class configuration (best viewed with zooming in). The orientation change of a robot corresponds to a rotational difference of a spherical image. (Color figure online)

4   Experimental Results

4.1   Network Setup and Training

Well designed training strategy is essential for good performance. In this paper, three models (as detailed in Table 1) are analyzed on the Spherical-Navi dataset. All of them share the common structure with the filter size equals to four.

For initialization, all the weights of neuron connections are initialized using the strategy in [14] and the biases are set to zero. During training, it would be wise to set a higher learning rate for models with PReLU activations than those with ReLU neurons. In our settings, the learning rate equals to 1e-5, 1e-4 for ReLU and PReLU respectively. And when the training loss first stops decreasing, all learning rates are divided by a scalar of ten. For better generalization, we use a mini-batch size of 10 and make a shuffle of all training images on every epoch.

The proposed algorithm is developed with the Torch7 package [16], which makes many efforts on improving the performance and efficacy of benchmark methods. The training procedure for all models listed in Table 1 can be finished within three days using an Intel Core-i7 3.4 GHz PC, and the CUDA version can be much shorter to less than 20 h with a Nvidia Titan X GPU. When testing, it takes 10ms for the onboard Nvidia Jetson TK1 to classify one image.

4.2   Quantitative Results and Discussion

Firstly, for a general view of the accuracy, Table 2 lists out the performance of all those models with the class number K varies. It demonstrates that we could use our approach in practice with a high confidence of larger than 86%.

As demonstrated in Table 2, among all those cases, our model 2 with BN performs best. Further, as the number of directions increase, all those methods' precision drops slightly. That is reasonable because when we have more classes, the chance of overlapping increases and then makes this problem more complicated. Besides, since the videos we captured is not guaranteed to be perfectly straightforward viewing, there might be some miss labelled images. This, in turn, can also affect the final precision.

Then, Fig. 4 gives a detailed classification result when $K = 7$. Since images of different classes are similar to each other in contents and varying with a slight difference of rotational degrees, neighbouring classes are more likely to be misclassified. That's why we have a higher value near the diagonal positions in

Table 2. Average classification results on our SphericalNavi dataset.

	[9]	Our model 1	Our model 2
3 classes	91.14%	92.64%	**94.30%**
5 classes	83.01%	84.82%	**93.07%**
7 classes	73.12%	72.36%	**86.41%**

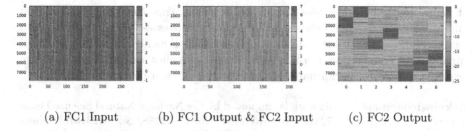

(a) FC1 Input   (b) FC1 Output & FC2 Input   (c) FC2 Output

Fig. 3. The feature responses of testing samples from different layers in model 2 (7-class case, best viewed in color). After the mapping of layer FC1(a2b) and FC2(b2c), samples are in a more discriminative subspace.

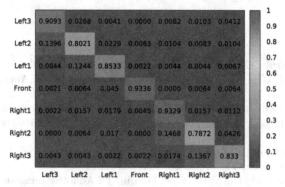

Fig. 4. The detailed classification accuracies of all the classes in our 7-direction case. The higher the diagonal values, the better classification performance.

the confusion matrix. It should also be noted that, when the robot is walking on a straight road, front-view images and rear-view images may be difficult to distinguish from each other. The same problem applies to left/right case. Consequently, there may be some samples that look like horizontally or vertically flipped. That's why we have a slightly high value in the upright corner.

Lastly, deep learning methods have made extraordinary success in many tasks mainly benefit from its great capability of mapping high dimensional data into discriminative feature spaces. Figure 3 gives an illustration of how features are mapped layer after layer to a compact subspace. Corresponding feature outputs of 8000 sample images from the last convolutional layer (Fig. 3(a)) and the fully connected layers (Fig. 3(b) and (c)) are shown together. As the dimension of features decreases from 288 to 7, those 8000 samples are getting warped into more compact groups and thus much easier for classifiers to make further predictions.

5   Conclusions

In this paper, we formulate the spherical camera based autonomous robot navigation task as an image classification problem. We then solve this problem with a CNN network trained on a set of specifically labeled images. This method of using raw panoramic information, without any time-consuming calibration and warping or global 3D virtual world building processes, works pretty well on mobile platforms with low computation resources. Benefited from the powerful capability of convolutional networks in solving classification problems, we have achieved impressive performance on our campus navigation experiments.

Acknowledgements. This work is supported by the National Natural Science Foundation of China (No. 61672429, No. 61502364, No. 61272288, No. 61231016), ShenZhen Science and Technology Foundation (JCYJ20160229172932237), Northwestern Polytechnical University (NPU) New AoXiang Star (No. G2015KY0301), Fundamental Research Funds for the Central Universities (No. 3102015AX007), NPU New People and Direction (No. 13GH014604).

References

1. Klein, G., Murray, D.: Parallel tracking and mapping for small AR workspaces. In: 6th IEEE and ACM International Symposium on Mixed and Augmented Reality, pp. 225–234 (2007)
2. Caruso, D., Engel, J., Cremers, D.: Large-scale direct slam for omnidirectional cameras. In: IEEE/RSJ International Conference on Intelligent Robots and Systems (IROS) (2015)
3. Hillel, A.B., Lerner, R., Levi, D., Raz, G.: Recent progress in road and lane detection: a survey. Mach. Vis. Appl. **25**, 727–745 (2014)
4. Liang, X., Wang, H., Chen, W., Guo, D., Liu, T.: Adaptive image-based trajectory tracking control of wheeled mobile robots with an uncalibrated fixed camera. IEEE Trans. Control Syst. Technol. **23**, 2266–2282 (2015)
5. Lu, K., Li, J., An, X., He, H.: Vision sensor-based road detection for field robot navigation. Sensors **15**, 29594–29617 (2015)
6. Chang, C.K., Siagian, C., Itti, L.: Mobile robot vision navigation & localization using gist and saliency. In: IEEE/RSJ International Conference on Intelligent Robots and Systems (IROS), pp. 4147–4154 (2010)
7. Pomerleau, D.A.: Efficient training of artificial neural networks for autonomous navigation. Neural Comput. **3**, 88–97 (1991)
8. Hadsell, R., Sermanet, P., Ben, J., Erkan, A., Scoffier, M., Kavukcuoglu, K., Muller, U., LeCun, Y.: Learning long-range vision for autonomous off-road driving. J. Field Robot. **26**, 120–144 (2009)
9. Giusti, A., Guzzi, J., Ciresan, D., He, F.L., Rodriguez, J.P., Fontana, F., Faessler, M., Forster, C., Schmidhuber, J., Di Caro, G., Scaramuzza, D., Gambardella, L.: A machine learning approach to visual perception of forest trails for mobile robots. IEEE Robot. Autom. Lett. **1**, 661–667 (2016)
10. Krizhevsky, A., Sutskever, I., Hinton, G.E.: Imagenet classification with deep convolutional neural networks. In: Advances in neural information processing systems, pp. 1097–1105 (2012)
11. Ran, L., Zhang, Y., Hua, G.: CANNET: context aware nonlocal convolutional networks for semantic image segmentation. In: IEEE International Conference on Image Processing (ICIP), pp. 4669–4673 (2015)
12. Girshick, R., Donahue, J., Darrell, T., Malik, J.: Region-based convolutional networks for accurate object detection and segmentation. IEEE Trans. Pattern Anal. Mach. Intell. (TPAMI) **38**, 142–158 (2016)

13. Nair, V., Hinton, G.E.: Rectified linear units improve restricted Boltzmann machines. In: Proceedings of the International Conference on Machine Learning (ICML), pp. 807–814 (2010)
14. He, K., Zhang, X., Ren, S., Sun, J.: Delving deep into rectifiers: surpassing human-level performance on imagenet classification. In: Proceedings of the IEEE Conference on Computer Vision and Pattern Recognition (CVPR), pp. 1026–1034 (2015)
15. Ioffe, S., Szegedy, C.: Batch normalization: accelerating deep network training by reducing internal covariate shift. In: Proceedings of the International Conference on Machine Learning (ICML), pp. 448–456 (2015)
16. Collobert, R., Kavukcuoglu, K., Farabet, C.: Torch7: a matlab-like environment for machine learning. In: BigLearn, NIPS Workshop. Number EPFL-CONF-192376 (2011)

Cascaded Tracking with Incrementally Learned Projections

Lianghua Huang$^{(\boxtimes)}$

Institute of Automation, Chinese Academy of Sciences, Beijing, China
huanglianghua@bit.edu.cn

Abstract. A convention in visual object tracking is to only favor the candidate with maximum similarity score and take it as the tracking result, while ignore the rest. However, surrounded samples also provide valuable information for target locating, and the combination of their votes can produce more stable results. In this paper, we have proposed a novel method based on the supervised descent method (SDM). We search for the target from multiple start positions and locate it with their votes. For evaluating each predicted descent direction, we have presented a confidence estimating scheme for SDM. To adapt the tracking model to appearance variations, we have further presented an incremental cascaded support vector regression (ICSVR) algorithm for model updating. Experimental results on a recent benchmark demonstrate the superior performance of our tracker against state-of-the-arts.

1 Introduction

As a fundamental subject in computer vision, visual object tracking plays a critical role in numerous applications including video surveillance, gait recognition, behavior analysis and robotics. Recent years have witnessed great progress in visual tracking [1–4]. Despite decades of studies, tracking is still a challenging task due to large appearance variations such as object deformation, occlusions, illumination variation and background clutter.

There are two main categories of tracking approaches: generative trackers and discriminative trackers. Generative approaches [5–8] take visual tracking as an appearance reconstruction problem. They mainly focus on the reconstruction model and online templates updating. Representative trackers are IVT [5] and sparse representation based trackers [6–8]. On the other hand, discriminative models [9–12] view tracking as a classification or regression task. They learn classifiers online with automatically labeled samples and locate the target with the candidate of maximum classification score. Some discriminative trackers are Struck [13], SCM [9], MEEM [14] and deep learning based methods [15–17]. Generally speaking, discriminative models are more robust against background clutters and thus they usually perform much better than generative ones.

A convention in tracking approaches, generative or discriminative, is to only favor the candidate with maximum similarity score, and afterwards the rest samples have no impact on the tracking result. However, surrounded samples also

© Springer Nature Singapore Pte Ltd. 2016
Z. Zhang and K. Huang (Eds.): IVS 2016, CCIS 664, pp. 56–64, 2016.
DOI: 10.1007/978-981-10-3476-3_7

provide valuable information for target locating, and the combination of their estimations can produce more stable results without increasing computational burden.

In this paper, we have proposed a novel method for visual tracking. Instead of basing the tracking result on one sample with maximum score, we approach the target from multiple surrounded candidates in a cascaded way by using the Supervised Descent Method (SDM) [18], and locate the target by searching for the most densely voted position. The SDM models the optimization for a non-linear problem with cascaded linear projections, which has been applied in various areas including facial landmark detection [18], extrinsic camera calibration [19] and visual tracking [20]. To provide an evaluation scheme for each predicted offset, we have presented a confidence estimation model for SDM which is learned from samples and updated online. To adapt the model to target appearance variations, we have further proposed an Incremental Cascaded Support Vector Regression (ICSVR) algorithm for model updating.

2   The Proposed Method

This section presents details on the proposed tracking model.

2.1   Cascaded Regression

The observation model in our approach is constructed based on the supervised descent method (SDM) [18], which learns the projection from features to descent directions in a cascaded way.

Specifically, for an object located at $\mathbf{s} \in \mathbb{R}^d$, we draw samples $\{\mathbf{s}_i\}_{i=1}^n$ around $\mathbf{s}$ to obtain training data $\{(\Delta\mathbf{s}_i, \phi_i)\}_{i=1}^n$, where $\phi_i \in \mathbb{R}^p$ denotes the extracted feature and $\Delta\mathbf{s}_i = \mathbf{s}_i - \mathbf{s}$ is the offset. The SDM learns the projections $\{\mathbf{R}_k \in \mathbb{R}^{d \times p}\}_{k=1}^C$ in a cascades way by iteratively optimizing the following C problems:

$$\min_{\mathbf{R}_k} \sum_i \|\Delta\mathbf{s}_i^k - \mathbf{R}_k\phi_i^k\|_2^2 + \lambda\|\mathbf{R}_k\|_2^2, \ k = 1, \cdots, C, \tag{1}$$

where k denotes the cascade index and $\mathbf{s}_i^1 = \mathbf{s}_i$, $\phi_i^1 = \phi_i$, $\Delta\mathbf{s}_i^k = \mathbf{s}_i^k - \mathbf{s}$, λ is a regularization parameter. With learned matrices $\{\mathbf{R}_k\}_{k=1}^C$, the iterative regression from a start state $\mathbf{s}_i^1$ to the estimated one $\hat{\mathbf{s}}_i = \mathbf{s}_i^{C+1}$ is formulated as:

$$\mathbf{s}_i^{k+1} = \mathbf{s}_i^k + \mathbf{R}_k\phi_i^k, \ k = 1, \cdots, C. \tag{2}$$

In our method, we use the support vector regression (SVR) algorithm for learning the projection matrices $\{\mathbf{R}_k\}_{k=1}^C$ since it is proven experimentally to be more robust against sample noise. Let $\mathbf{r}_{kj}$ denotes the jth row of $\mathbf{R}_k$, and s_{ij}^k denotes the jth entry of $\mathbf{s}_i^k$, the cascaded SVR is formulated as:

$$\min_{\mathbf{r}_{kj}, \xi_{ki}, \xi_{ki}^*} \frac{1}{2}\|\mathbf{r}_{kj}\|_2^2 + \eta_1 \sum_{i=1}^{n}(\xi_{ki} + \xi_{ki}^*),$$

$$s.t.\ \ \mathbf{r}_{kj} \cdot \phi_{ki} - \Delta s_{ij}^k \leq \varepsilon_1 + \xi_{ki},$$

$$\Delta s_{ij}^k - \mathbf{r}_{kj} \cdot \phi_{ki} \leq \varepsilon_1 + \xi_{ki}^*,$$

$$\xi_{ki},\ \xi_{ki}^* \geq 0$$

$$i = 1, \cdots, n,\ \ k = 1, \cdots, C \qquad (3)$$

where η_1 is a regularization factor, ξ_{ki}, ξ_{ki}^* are slack variables and ε_1 is a preset margin which is fixed to $\varepsilon_1 = 5$ empirically in our experiments.

2.2   Confidence Evaluation

Despite the effectiveness of SDM, its main drawback is the lack of a mechanism for indicating how reliable an offset prediction is. In this section, we present a confidence evaluation scheme for SDM.

In training stage, if one regress iteration pulls a sample closer to the groundtruth, we say that the sample is more credible and vice versa. Based on the idea, we propose to learn an extra set of projection matrices $\{\mathbf{Q}_k \in \mathbf{R}^{1 \times p}\}_{k=1}^C$ for confidence evaluation. We take the ratio of overlap rates before and after regression $\theta_i^k = (o_i^{k+1})^2 / o_i^k$ (where o_i^k denotes the overlap between s_i^k and s) as the label to train $\{\mathbf{Q}_k\}_{k=1}^C$:

$$\min_{\mathbf{Q}_k, \xi_{ki}, \xi_{ki}^*} \frac{1}{2}\|\mathbf{Q}_k\|_2^2 + \eta_2 \sum_{i=1}^{n}(\xi_{ki} + \xi_{ki}^*),$$

$$s.t.\ \ \mathbf{Q}_k \cdot \phi_{ki} - \theta_i^k \leq \varepsilon_2 + \xi_{ki}$$

$$\theta_i^k - \mathbf{Q}_k \cdot \phi_{ki} \leq \varepsilon_2 + \xi_{ki}^*$$

$$\xi_{ki},\ \xi_{ki}^* \geq 0,$$

$$i = 1, \cdots, n,\ \ k = 1, \cdots, C \qquad (4)$$

When testing, the reliability c_i of each sample is computed as:

$$c_i = \prod_{k=1}^{C} \theta_i^k,\ \ k = 1, \cdots, C. \qquad (5)$$

2.3   Target Locating

When locating target in a new frame, we sample around the last estimated position to obtain m candidates $\{\mathbf{s}_i, \phi_i\}_{i=1}^m$. With the learned cascaded model, we iteratively pull each sample $\mathbf{s}_i$ to the target location:

$$\mathbf{s}_i^{k+1} = \mathbf{s}_i^k + \mathbf{R}_k \phi_i,\ \ k = 1, \cdots, C. \qquad (6)$$

After C iterations, we obtain all the estimated states $\hat{\mathbf{s}}_i = \mathbf{s}_i^{C+1}$. Intuitively, the most densely voted position is more likely to be the target location. In our method, we use the dominant set [21] algorithm for locating the voting center.

The dominant set algorithm computes sample weights w_i by optimizing:

$$\max_{\mathbf{w}} \ \mathbf{w}^{\mathrm{T}} \mathbf{A} \mathbf{w},$$

$$\text{s.t. } \mathbf{w} \in \Lambda, \tag{7}$$

where $\Lambda = \{\mathbf{w} \in \mathbb{R}^m : \mathbf{w} > \mathbf{0} \text{ and } \mathbf{e}^{\mathrm{T}} \mathbf{w} = 1\}$, $\mathbf{e} \in \mathbb{R}^m$ is a vector of all 1s, $\mathbf{A} \in \mathbb{R}^{m \times m}$ is an affinity matrix with each entry $A_{ij} = \exp\left(\frac{\|\hat{\mathbf{s}}_i - \hat{\mathbf{s}}_j\|_2^2}{2\sigma_A^2}\right)$ representing the similarity between $\mathbf{s}_i^{C+1}$ and $\mathbf{s}_j^{C+1}$, σ_A is a scaling factor which is set to the median value of all entries in $\mathbf{A}$. Finally, the estimated target location is obtained by:

$$\hat{\mathbf{s}} = \sum_i w_i \hat{\mathbf{s}}_i. \tag{8}$$

Taking sample confidences c_i into consideration, we slightly modify the affinity matrix $\mathbf{A}$ as:

$$A_{ij}^* = c_i \cdot c_j \cdot A_{ij}. \tag{9}$$

The rest voting process is the same as described before.

3 Updating Scheme

To adapt the model to target appearance variations, we propose an Incremental Cascaded Support Vector Regression (ICSVR) algorithm for online model updating.

Note that the Support Vector Regression (SVR) problem with training samples $\{\mathbf{x}_i, y_i\}_{i=1}^l$ and preset margin ε is equivalent to a Support Vector Classification (SVC) problem with modified training data $\{(\mathbf{z}_i, 1)\}_{i=1}^l$ and $\{(\mathbf{z}_i, -1)\}_{i=l+1}^{2l}$, where $\mathbf{z}_i = (\mathbf{x}_i^{\mathrm{T}}, y_i + \varepsilon)^{\mathrm{T}}$ for $i = 1, \cdots, l$ and $\mathbf{z}_i = (\mathbf{x}_i^{\mathrm{T}}, y_i - \varepsilon)^{\mathrm{T}}$ for $i = l+1, \cdots, 2l$:

$$\min_{\mathbf{w}, \boldsymbol{\xi}} \ \frac{1}{2} \|\mathbf{w}\|_2^2 + \eta \sum_{i=1}^{2l} \xi_i,$$

$$\text{s.t. } (\mathbf{w} \cdot \mathbf{z}_i) \geq 1 - \xi_i, \ i = 1, \cdots, l$$

$$-(\mathbf{w} \cdot \mathbf{z}_i) \geq 1 - \xi_i, \ i = l+1, \cdots, 2l,$$

$$\xi_i \geq 0, \ i = 1, \cdots, 2l \tag{10}$$

where η is a regularization parameter. In this way, the incremental learning of SVR can also be implemented by online SVC with slightly modified training samples. We use the work proposed in [22] as the SVC updater in our approach.

As for the cascaded process, in training stage, we collect samples and overlap rates accross C cascades, and train SVRs with samples in corresponding cascades.

4   Experiments

We evaluate our tracking approach on a publicly available benchmark [23], which contains 51 challenging sequences, and compare the performance with 30 trackers, where 28 of which are recommended by [23] including Struck [13], SCM [9], TLD [24], VTD [25], CT [26] and ALSA [27], while the KCF [28] and DSST [29] are recent state-of-the-art trackers.

4.1   Implementation Details

The proposed approach is implemented on MATLAB R2015b and run on a 2.6 GHz Intel Core i5 CPU with 8 GB memory. The code without optimization runs at 3.5 fps in average. Each sampled image is converted to grayscale and normalized to 32×32, then HOG feature is extracted on it with bin size 4. For simplicity, we only estimate the target position $\mathbf{s} = \{x, y\}$ and assume the scale and angle of the target stay the same during tracking. In training stage, we sample 200 images around the target with sample radius $r_1 = 8$. $C = 3$ cascades of SVR are trained with regularization parameters $\eta_1 = 0.001, \eta_2 = 0.001$. ε_1 is set to 5 and ε_2 is set to 1. When testing, 400 images are sampled around the last estimated target location with sample radius $r_2 = 20$. The model updating is performed each $T = 5$ frames. All the parameters are fixed for different sequences for fair comparison.

4.2   Overall Performance

The overall performance of our method on the benchmark [23] is illustrated in Fig. 1. We apply the precision plot and the success plot for comparing

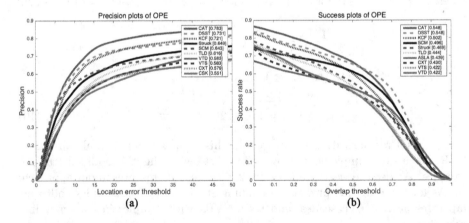

Fig. 1. Overall performance of 30 state-of-the-art trackers and our tracker on the benchmark. For clarity, only top 10 trackers are illustrated. (a) Precision scores. (b) Success scores.

performance between different trackers. The precision plot indicates the percentage of frames whose estimated location is within the given threshold distance to the ground truth, while the success plot demonstrates the ratios of successful frames whose overlap rate is larger than the given threshold. The precision score is decided by the score on a selected threshold (20 pixel), and the success score is evaluated by the Area Under Curve (AUC) of each plot. For clarity, only top 10 trackers are illustrated on both plots.

As can be seen from Fig. 1(a) and (b), our method obtains superior performance against others. In the precision plot, our tracker outperforms DSST by 5.2 % and outperforms KCF by 6.2 %. In the success plot, our tracker performs as good as DSST and 4.6 % better than KCF. The DSST employs an accurate scale estimation scheme while our tracker does not estimate the target scale, which makes the DSST obtains competitive performance in the success plot. Overall, our tracker performs competitive or better than state-of-the-arts in terms of both the location accuracy and overlap precision.

The superior performance of our tracker validates the effectiveness of sample voting and the cascaded support vector regression scheme. The cascaded process models the non-linear mapping from features to offsets with iterative linear regressions. In addition, the proposed Incremental Cascaded Support Vector Regression (ICSVR) algorithm provides an effective way for robust model updating, which contributes greatly to the stability of long term tracking.

4.3   Component Validation

This section carries out experiments for verifying the contributions of different components in our method. Three components are evaluated in this section: the dominant set voting, the sample confidence evaluation and the incremental learning of cascaded SVR.

Figure 2(a) compares precision scores among trackers using different voting methods. CAT-DS, CAT-MED and CAT-MS denote the trackers using dominant set voting, (weighted) median voting and (weighted) mean shift voting schemes respectively, where the weights are computed as described in Sect. 2.2.

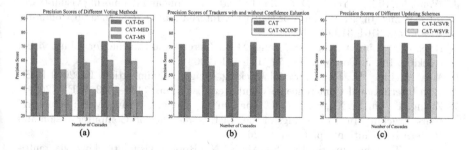

Fig. 2. Validations of different components. (a) Precision scores with and without confidence evaluation. (b) Precision scores of different updating schemes. (c) Precision scores of different voting methods.

As can be seen from Fig. 2(a), CAT-DS significantly outperforms CAT-MED and CAT-MS, which indicates that the dominant set voting is more stable in finding the most densely voted place.

Figure 2(b) compares precision scores between trackers with and without confidence evaluation, namely the CAT and the CAT-NCONF trackers. There's a striking disparity between their scores, which indicates that the sample confidence evaluation is an indispensable part in our method.

Figure 2(c) compares precision scores between trackers using different updating schemes. CAT-ICSVR denotes the tracker using the proposed Incremental Cascaded Support Vector Regression (ICSVR) updating scheme while the CT-WSVR denotes the one using weighted parameter updating scheme (with forgetting factor $\lambda = 0.1$). As illustrated in Fig. 2(c), CAT-ICSVR outperforms CAT-WSVR by 8.8 % when the cascade number is set to 3, which indicates the significant contribution of ICSVR updating algorithm on the tracking performance.

Besides, we can see from the figures that, as the cascade number increases, the performance of our tracker (CAT) steadily rises and reaches the top at 3 cascade, then slightly declines when the number gets larger. This trend reflects the mechanism of SDM and its effectiveness. The SDM models the optimization for a non-linear problem with cascaded linear projections. When the cascade number grows from 1 to 3, the precision score rises since the model fits the data better. Whereas the performance decreases afterwards, which indicates that the SDM gets overfitting on the training data when the model becomes more complex.

References

1. Smeulders, A.W., Chu, D.M., Cucchiara, R., Calderara, S., Dehghan, A., Shah, M.: Visual tracking: an experimental survey. IEEE Trans. Patt. Anal. Mach. Intell. **36**, 1442–1468 (2014)
2. Yang, H., Shao, L., Zheng, F., Wang, L., Song, Z.: Recent advances and trends in visual tracking: a review. Neurocomputing **74**, 3823–3831 (2011)
3. Yilmaz, A., Javed, O., Shah, M.: Object tracking: a survey. ACM Comput. Surv. (CSUR) **38**, 13 (2006)
4. Wang, N., Shi, J., Yeung, D.Y., Jia, J.: Understanding and diagnosing visual tracking systems. In: Proceedings of the IEEE International Conference on Computer Vision, pp. 3101–3109 (2015)
5. Ross, D.A., Lim, J., Lin, R.S., Yang, M.H.: Incremental learning for robust visual tracking. Int. J. Comput. Vis. **77**, 121–141 (2008)
6. Mei, X., Ling, H.: Robust visual tracking using l1 minimization. In: 2009 IEEE 12th International Conference on Computer Vision, pp. 1436–1443. IEEE (2009)
7. Zhang, T., Liu, S., Xu, C., Yan, S., Ghanem, B., Ahuja, N., Yang, M.H.: Structural sparse tracking. In: Proceedings of the IEEE Conference on Computer Vision and Pattern Recognition, pp. 150–158 (2015)
8. Zhang, T., Ghanem, B., Liu, S., Ahuja, N.: Robust visual tracking via multi-task sparse learning. In: 2012 IEEE Conference on Computer Vision and Pattern Recognition (CVPR), pp. 2042–2049. IEEE (2012)

9. Zhong, W., Lu, H., Yang, M.H.: Robust object tracking via sparsity-based collaborative model. In: 2012 IEEE Conference on Computer Vision and Pattern Recognition (CVPR), pp. 1838–1845. IEEE (2012)
10. Yao, R., Shi, Q., Shen, C., Zhang, Y., Hengel, A.: Part-based visual tracking with online latent structural learning. In: Proceedings of the IEEE Conference on Computer Vision and Pattern Recognition, pp. 2363–2370 (2013)
11. Liu, B., Huang, J., Kulikowski, C., Yang, L.: Robust visual tracking using local sparse appearance model and k-selection. IEEE Trans. Patt. Anal. Mach. Intell. **35**, 2968–2981 (2013)
12. Jia, X., Lu, H., Yang, M.H.: Visual tracking via adaptive structural local sparse appearance model. In: 2012 IEEE Conference on Computer Vision and Pattern Recognition (CVPR), pp. 1822–1829. IEEE(2012)
13. Hare, S., Saffari, A., Torr, P.H.S.: Struck: structured output tracking with kernels. In: 2011 IEEE International Conference on Computer Vision (ICCV), pp. 263–270 (2011)
14. Zhang, J., Ma, S., Sclaroff, S.: MEEM: robust tracking via multiple experts using entropy minimization. In: Fleet, D., Pajdla, T., Schiele, B., Tuytelaars, T. (eds.) ECCV 2014. LNCS, vol. 8694, pp. 188–203. Springer, Cham (2014). doi:10.1007/978-3-319-10599-4_13
15. Wang, N., Yeung, D.Y.: Learning a deep compact image representation for visual tracking. In: Advances in Neural Information Processing Systems, pp. 809–817 (2013)
16. Nam, H., Han, B.: Learning multi-domain convolutional neural networks for visual tracking. In: The IEEE Conference on Computer Vision and Pattern Recognition (CVPR) (2016)
17. Wang, N., Li, S., Gupta, A., Yeung, D.Y.: Transferring rich feature hierarchies for robust visual tracking. arXiv preprint arxiv:1501.04587 (2015)
18. Xiong, X., Torre, F.: Supervised descent method and its applications to face alignment. In: Proceedings of the IEEE Conference on Computer Vision and Pattern Recognition, pp. 532–539 (2013)
19. Xiong, X., la Torre, F.D.: Global supervised descent method. In: 2015 IEEE Conference on Computer Vision and Pattern Recognition (CVPR), pp. 2664–2673 (2015)
20. Wang, X., Valstar, M., Martinez, B., Khan, M.H., Pridmore, T.: Tric-track: tracking by regression with incrementally learned cascades. In: IEEE International Conference on Computer Vision, pp. 4337–4345 (2015)
21. Massimiliano, P., Marcello, P.: Dominant sets and pairwise clustering. IEEE Trans. Patt. Anal. Mach. Intell. **29**, 167–172 (2007)
22. Wang, Z., Vucetic, S.: Online training on a budget of support vector machines using twin prototypes. Statistical Analysis and Data Mining **3**, 149–169 (2010)
23. Wu, Y., Lim, J., Yang, M.H.: Online object tracking: a benchmark. In: Proceedings of the IEEE Conference on Computer Vision and Pattern Recognition, pp. 2411–2418 (2013)
24. Kalal, Z., Mikolajczyk, K., Matas, J.: Tracking-learning-detection. IEEE Trans. Pattern Anal. Mach. Intell. **34**, 1409–1422 (2012)
25. Kwon, J., Lee, K.M.: Visual tracking decomposition. In: IEEE Conference on Computer Vision and Pattern Recognition, pp. 1269–1276 (2010)
26. Zhang, K., Zhang, L., Yang, M.-H.: Real-time compressive tracking. In: Fitzgibbon, A., Lazebnik, S., Perona, P., Sato, Y., Schmid, C. (eds.) ECCV 2012. LNCS, vol. 7574, pp. 864–877. Springer, Berlin (2012). doi:10.1007/978-3-642-33712-3_62

27. Jia, X.: Visual tracking via adaptive structural local sparse appearance model. In: IEEE Conference on Computer Vision and Pattern Recognition, pp. 1822–1829 (2012)

28. Henriques, J.F., Caseiro, R., Martins, P., Batista, J.: High-speed tracking with kernelized correlation filters. IEEE Trans. Patt. Anal. Mach. Intell. **37**, 583–596 (2014)

29. Danelljan, M., Hger, G., Khan, F.S., Felsberg, M.: Accurate scale estimation for robust visual tracking. In: British Machine Vision Conference (2015)

Tracking Multiple Players in Beach Volleyball Videos

Xiaokang Jiang, Zheng Liu, and Yunhong Wang[✉]

The Laboratory of Intelligent Recognition and Image Processing,
School of Computer Science and Engineering,
Beihang University, Beijing 100191, China
yhwang@buaa.edu.cn

Abstract. Multi-object tracking has been a difficult problem in recent years, especially in complex scenes such as player tracking in sports videos. Player movements are often complex and abrupt. In this paper, we focus on the problem of tracking multiple players in beach volleyball videos. To handle the difficulties of player tracking, we follow the popular tracking-by-detection framework in multi-object tracking and adopt the multiple hypotheses tracking (MHT) algorithm to solve the data association problem. To improve the efficiency of the MHT, we use motion information from Kalman filter and train an online appearance model of each track hypothesis. An auxiliary particle filter method is adopted to handle the missing detection problem. Furthermore, we obtain the significant performance on our beach volleyball datasets, which demonstrate the effectiveness and efficiency of the proposed method.

1 Introduction

With the explosive growth of various video data, automatic video processing has become more and more important in order to reduce the manual effort for video analysis. Among all kinds of video data, sports videos captured from different kinds of matches, such as football, basketball and volleyball has attracted a lot of research interests, due to their huge popularity and tremendous commercial value.

Compared with multiple object tracking (MOT) in other scenes, multiple player tracking in sports video is much more difficult due to the following reasons: (1) players in the same team are always visually similar, making the appearance information less discriminative and unreliable; (2) sports players often interact with others in complex ways and (3) the occlusions are much more frequent and severe. All of these issues together have posed quite a great challenge to the tracking system, which requires not only reliable observations but also a sophisticated tracking strategy to make the system robust.

Recent progress on Multi-Object Tracking (MOT) has focused on the tracking-by-detection strategy, where object detections from a category detector are linked to form trajectories of the targets. In this work, we aim to track multiple highly dynamic and interactive players in beach volleyball videos. Firstly, we follow the popular tracking-by-detection framework in MOT. Concretely, we employ the DPM [1] detector to get the detection results. Next, to solve the data association problem, the classical multiple hypotheses tracking (MHT) algorithm [2] is adopted.

Z. Zhang and K. Huang (Eds.): IVS 2016, CCIS 664, pp. 65–71, 2016.
DOI: 10.1007/978-981-10-3476-3_8

The contributions of this paper lie in the following three-fold: (1) We train multiple online appearance models to improve the efficiency and accuracy of the MHT tacking method; (2) An auxiliary color-based particle filter is applied to handle missing detections; (3) We analyze the robustness of the method, in particular the influence of each part of the tracking system.

The paper is structured as follows: After discussing related work in the following section, Sect. 3 describes the details of MHT. Section 4 talks about how the online appearance model and the particle filter help improving the tracking result. Section 5 presents experiments and analyzes the performance of our method.

2   Related Work

As object detection has made impressive improvements in recent years, MOT has focused on the tracking-by-detection strategy. Different from the data association-based tracking approaches, there are many methods use the detection results from a probabilistic inference perspective. A Kalman filter [3] is an early representative method. Then based on sequential Monte Carlo sampling, particle filters [4] gained much attention because of their simplicity, generality, and extensibility in a wide range of challenging applications.

There are many papers about multiple player detection and tracking in sports video. In [5], Huang et al. first detected the players and ball based on extracted foreground and then performed shape analysis to remove false alarms. To conquer the problem of complex multiple object interactions with overlaps and ambiguities, Okuma et al. [6] used an offline boosted particle filter to track each player in a mixture representation.

However, probabilistic inference methods cannot solve the highly dynamic and interactive players in sports videos, due to the severe occlusions and abrupt movements of players. So recently many methods have posed multi-object tracking as data association. Majority of the batch methods formulates MOT as a global optimization problem in graph-based representation, due to their computational efficiency and optimality. The problem of associating tracklets has been investigated using a variety of method, such as the Hungarian algorithm [7], k-shortest paths [8], cost-flow networks [9] and discrete-continuous optimization [10]. Kim et al. [11] follow the classical formulation in [2] and corporate the appearance modeling with MHT. We also apply the MHT in multiple player tracking of beach volleyball.

3   Multiple Hypotheses Tracking Algorithm

In the MHT algorithm, observations are localized bounding boxes. Generally, the MHT framework consists of the following five steps.

3.1   Track Tree Construction and Updating

A track tree encapsulates multiple hypotheses starting from a single observation. At each frame, a new track tree is constructed for each observation. Previously existing track trees are also updated with observations from the current frame.

3.2 Gating

To predict the tracking area of each track hypothesis, the motion information is taken into consideration. The Kalman filter is used to predict the location of the target. Then the Mahalanobis distance d^2 between the predict location and a new observation is calculated to decide whether to update a particular trajectory. The distance threshold d_{th} determines the size of the gating area.

3.3 Tracking Score

Each track hypothesis is associated with a track score. The lth track's score at frame k is defined as follows:

$$S^l(k) = \omega_{mot}S^l_{mot}(k) + \omega_{app}S^l_{app}(k) \tag{1}$$

where $S^l_{mot}(k)$ and $S^l_{app}(k)$ are the motion and appearance scores, and ω_{mot}, ω_{app} are the weights that control the contribution of the location measurement and the appearance measurement to the track score, respectively. The motion and the appearance score are calculated like the formulation in [11].

3.4 Global Hypothesis Formation

Given the set of trees that contains all trajectory hypotheses of all targets, we wish to determine the most likely global hypothesis. We follow the formulation in [2]. The global hypothesis formation problem is formulated as a Maximum Weighted Independent Set (MWIS) problem.

3.5 Track Tree Pruning

In order to avoid the exponential growth of the graph size, the pruning step is applied for MHT. We adopt the standard N-scan pruning approach. Figure 1 shows an example.

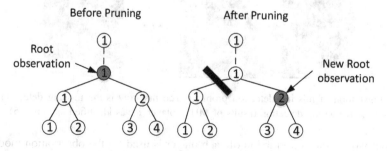

Fig. 1. An example of N-scan pruning ($N = 2$)

We also set a threshold B_{th} to retain a track tree's branches based on its track score. Only the top B_{th} branches are kept. This is because the number of players in beach volleyball is static. In this way, we can make pruning more efficient.

4   Online Appearance Model and Particle Filter Method

4.1   Online Appearance Model

Considering the complexity of beach volleyball player tracking, in addition to the motion estimates method, we build an online appearance model of each target. We utilize the convolutional neural network features trained on the ImageNet+PASCAL VOC dataset in [12]. The 4096-dimensional feature for each observation box is extracted. To save the time and space, a principal component analysis (PCA) is then performed to reduce the dimensionality of the features. In the experiments we take the first 256 principal components. We follow the multi-output regularized least squares framework [13].

4.2   An Auxiliary Particle Filter

In the MHT framework, if there is a sequence of missing observations, the corresponding track hypothesis will be deleted from the hypothesis space. This may cause false tracking results, which is resulted from missing detections of the detector. Figure 2 shows an example.

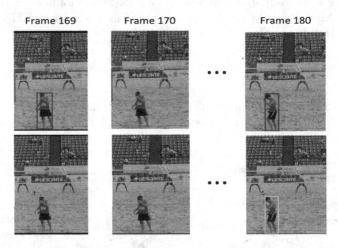

Fig. 2. Illustration of missing detection problem. The first row is the missing detection. The second row is the wrong detection results of MHT (player 1 was identified as player 5)

In our work, color information of each player is used for the observation model in the particle filter framework. We take the HSV color space of each player and create a one dimensional histogram containing $N_H * N_S$ bins and N_V bins appended.

Firstly, the color histogram of each player is calculated on the first frame based on the bounding box with high detection confidential scores. When a bounding box has no adjacent boxes on the next frame, we assume that the missing detection problem happens. Then a similarity matric between the bounding box and players is calculated. If the bounding box is similar to one of the players, a particle filter is initialized to predict the position of the bounding box in the next frame. The particle filter continues until a new bounding box from the detector is found around the predict position. In this way, we can avoid false tracking results in some degrees.

5 Experiments

We evaluate the performance of our framework on a Beach Volleyball Dataset. There are 200 frames labeled for beach volleyball games.

The entire system is implemented in Matlab on the platform of Linux. The popular DPM detector, which is publicly available, is used to get bounding boxes of players. The model trained on the INRIA Person dataset is applied. In Fig. 3, we show some tracking output on our beach volleyball datasets. We can see that our tracking method can handle the occlusion problem well. For comparison, we choose the state-of-the-art MOT method proposed in [11]. The same DPM detector is used in our dataset.

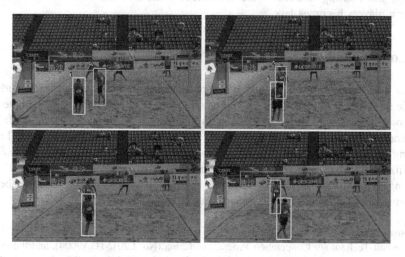

Fig. 3. Tracking output on the beach volleyball dataset.

Algorithm Parameters: In the proposed tracking algorithm, as to MHT, we set $\omega_{mot} = 0.2$ and $\omega_{app} = 0.8$ considering that the appearance model plays a more important role. And the max number of each track tree's branches B_{th} is set to 10. The dummy numbers threshold $N_{miss} = 15$. N about the N-scan is set to 7 in our experiment. And the Mahalanobis distance $d_{th} = 12$. As to the particle filter method, the particle number of each target is set to 50. As to color histogram, we set $N_H = 10$, $N_S = 10$ and

$N_V = 10$. The smaller number of particles means faster speed, while may result in lower accuracy.

Evaluation: We follow the current evaluation protocols in [14] for visual multi-target tracking. The multiple object tracking accuracy (MOTA), multiple object tracking precision (MOTP). The number of false positives (FP), the number of false negatives (FN), the total number of identity switches (IDS) are also reported.

Table 1 shows the results about our method and the MHT_DAM method on the beach volleyball dataset. We also list the results about the method without the help of the auxiliary particle filter for comparison.

Table 1. Results on the beach volleyball dataset

Method	MOTA	MOTP	FP	FN	IDS
MHT_DAM [11]	64.3%	66.7%	36.3%	2.6%	2
Ours(without PF)	64.5%	67.3%	35.1%	2.6%	2
Ours	67.2%	70.7%	29.7%	0.3%	1

From Table 1, we can see that the MOTA and MOTP of our method are better than the MHT_DAM and method without particle filtering. The FN becomes smaller because the missing detections are alleviated. What's more, the identity switches between players becomes less.

6   Conclusion

We have proposed a novel method based on the tracking-by-detection framework to handle the MOT problem for beach volleyball videos. The MHT method is adopted to overcome the false positive detections in the data association procedure. Online appearance models are trained to improve the efficiency and accuracy of the MHT tacking method. To alleviate the missing detection problem, a color-based particle filter is utilized. Through this way, better observations are provided for multiple player tracking. Experimental results demonstrate that the proposed method achieves better performance, compared with the state-of-the-art approaches.

Acknowledgments. This work was supported in part by the Hong Kong, Macao and Taiwan Science and Technology Cooperation Program of China (No. L2015TGA9004), and the Foundation for Innovative Research Groups of the National Natural Science Foundation of China (No. 61573045, 61421003).

References

1. Felzenszwalb, P.F., et al.: Object detection with discriminatively trained part-based models. IEEE Trans. Pattern Anal. Mach. Intell. **32**(9), 1627–1645 (2010)

2. Papageorgiou, D.J., Salpukas, M.R.: The maximum weight independent set problem for data association in multiple hypothesis tracking. In: Hirsch, M.J., Commander, C.W., Pardalos, P.M., Murphey, R. (eds.) Optimization and Cooperative Control Strategies. LNCIS, vol. 381, pp. 235–255. Springer, Heidelberg (2009). doi:10.1007/978-3-540-88063-9_15

3. Kalman, R.E.: An introduction to Kalman filter. TR 95-041, University of North Carolina at Chapel Hill, Department of Computer Science (1995)

4. Isard, M., Blake, A.: Condensation—conditional density propagation for visual tracking. Int. J. Comput. Vis. **29**(1), 5–28 (1998)

5. Huang, Yu., Llach, J., Bhagavathy, S.: Players and ball detection in soccer videos based on color segmentation and shape analysis. In: Sebe, N., Liu, Y., Zhuang, Y., Huang, Thomas, S. (eds.) MCAM 2007. LNCS, vol. 4577, pp. 416–425. Springer, Heidelberg (2007). doi:10. 1007/978-3-540-73417-8_50

6. Okuma, K., Taleghani, A., Freitas, N., Little, James, J., Lowe, David, G.: A boosted particle filter: multitarget detection and tracking. In: Pajdla, T., Matas, J. (eds.) ECCV 2004. LNCS, vol. 3021, pp. 28–39. Springer, Heidelberg (2004). doi:10.1007/978-3-540-24670-1_3

7. Bae, S.-H., Yoon, K.-J.: Robust online multi-object tracking based on tracklet confidence and online discriminative appearance learning. In: 2014 IEEE Conference on Computer Vision and Pattern Recognition. IEEE (2014)

8. Berclaz, J., et al.: Multiple object tracking using k-shortest paths optimization. IEEE Trans. Pattern Anal. Mach. Intell. **33**(9), 1806–1819 (2011)

9. Butt, A.A., Collins R.T.: Multi-target tracking by lagrangian relaxation to min-cost network flow. In: Proceedings of the IEEE Conference on Computer Vision and Pattern Recognition (2013)

10. Andriyenko, A., Schindler, K., Roth, S.: Discrete-continuous optimization for multi-target tracking. In: 2012 IEEE Conference on Computer Vision and Pattern Recognition (CVPR). IEEE (2012)

11. Kim, C., et al.: Multiple hypothesis tracking revisited. In: Proceedings of the IEEE International Conference on Computer Vision (2015)

12. Krizhevsky, A., Sutskever, I., Hinton, G.E.: Imagenet classification with deep convolutional neural networks. In: Advances in Neural Information Processing Systems (2012)

13. Li, F., et al.: Video segmentation by tracking many figure-ground segments. In: Proceedings of the IEEE International Conference on Computer Vision (2013)

14. Bernardin, K., Stiefelhagen, R.: Evaluating multiple object tracking performance: the CLEAR MOT metrics. EURASIP J. Image and Video Process. **2008**(1), 1–10 (2008)

Multi-object Tracking Within
Air-Traffic-Control Surveillance Videos

Yan Li[✉], Siyuan Chen, and Xiaolong Jiang

Beijing Key Laboratory for Network-Based Cooperative
Air Traffic Management, School of Electronic and Information Engineering,
Beihang University, Beijing 100191, People's Republic of China
liyansjtu@163.com

Abstract. In this paper, we strive to settle Multi-object tracking (MOT) problem within Air-Traffic-Control (ATC) surveillance videos. The uniqueness and challenges of the specific problem at hand is two-fold. Firstly, the targets within ATC surveillance videos are small and demonstrate homogeneous appearance. Secondly, the number of targets within the tracking scene undergoes severe variations results from multiple reasons. To solve such a problem, we propose a method that combines the advantages of fast association algorithm and local adjustment technique under a general energy minimization framework. Specifically, a comprehensive and discriminative energy function is established to measure the probability of hypothetical movement of targets, and the optimal output of the function yields to the most responsible target state configuration. Extensive experiments prove the effectiveness of our method on this new dataset.

1 Introduction

Multi-object tracking (MOT) has been widely studied in recent years and resulted in a fruitful selection of literature [1–6]. In this paper, however, a more specific and complex MOT problem is resolved. Particularly, we try to design a method to perform reliable tracking of multiple identical small targets within ATC surveillance videos. The realization of such a method is significant as it lays solid foundation for the development computer-aided ATC.

Compared with previous MOT datasets, the specialty and complexity of the ATC surveillance videos is two-fold. Firstly, the reasons for targets number variations are diversified. Besides the common way where target entering and leaving the margin of the scene may lead to varying target number, aircrafts targets within the ATC surveillance videos can also emerge or disappear in the center of the scene (Fig. 1). This phenomenon results from the fact that the airport should be the head of departing aircrafts' trajectories or the tail of approaching aircrafts' trajectories. In application, this uncommon behavior of the targets may bring about extra difficulty in realizing reliable tracking. Secondly, as the ATC surveillance videos cover a vast range of field containing massive number of objects, thus the targets at concern are usually small-sized which provide limited appearance cues. Consequently, the appearances of different targets are highly identical. The combination of the above two issues are prone to result

© Springer Nature Singapore Pte Ltd. 2016
Z. Zhang and K. Huang (Eds.): IVS 2016, CCIS 664, pp. 72–80, 2016.
DOI: 10.1007/978-981-10-3476-3_9

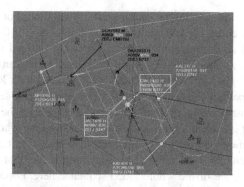

Fig. 1. Unusual way of targets emerging and disappearing within Air-traffic-control Surveillance Video. The blue one is going to landing and the orange one and the green one have just taken off. (Color figure online)

in spurious association of an approaching aircraft with a departure aircraft, if the traditional multiple target tracking methods are applied.

To cope with these difficulties, the method proposed in this work follows the tracking-by-detection (TBD) strategy in consideration of its ability of identifying new appearing. Nonetheless, this strategy is still inadequate to handle the possible identity mislabel caused by the entering and leaving targets. Consequently, an energy minimization [5] framework is also constructed in the proposed work, where a tailored energy function is designed to resolve our special tracking problem. Specifically, error associations between approaching and departing airplanes are specially penalized by a relative distance difference energy term. In addition, proper initial value and the corresponding energy optimization details are also introduced to make our method more efficiently.

The main contribution of the proposed work is three-fold: Firstly, a new energy function aiming at our special ATC surveillance videos is proposed. Secondly, a proper initial value for energy-based method is selected for homogeneous motion targets tracking; Thirdly, satisfactory experiment results are achieved on challenging ATC surveillance videos.

The rest of this paper is organized as follows. After related work is discussed in Sect. 2, the proposed method is elaborated in Sect. 3. Section 4 demonstrates the experiment results on our ATC surveillance datasets. Section 5 draws the conclusions of the proposed MOT approach.

2   Related Work

The proposed method in this work follows the TBD framework. As the name suggests, a TBD method usually consists of two components: target detection and data association modules. Depending on the temporal operation strategy, TBD methods can be further categorized as local or global methods. The local methods generate tracking results frame-by-frame or batch-by-batch, using the detection outputs obtained from only a limited-length time window at each round of operation. For the local methods, such as bi-partite matching [7] and multiple frames matching [8], data association is typically formed into an optimization problem where the optimal affinity matching is computed. However, as this line of method only uses a fraction of frames at each association, thus it might not be robust enough when faced with long-time occlusion and intricate motion pattern because of the lack of comprehensive sequential cues. As a result, mainstream methods at present are all global, where the tracking result is generated on basis of the detection responses acquired from the whole video sequence. Similar to the local methods, the global methods also transform the problem of association into optimization, yet the difference resides in the fact that the optimization is only executed in the scale of the whole video sequence here. Popular global methods involve optimization schemes such as network flows [9], k-shortest paths [10], maximum weight independent set [11], etc. All of these strategies usually employ a graph model that selects a subset of nodes and edges to maximize similarity of hypotheses.

In addition, some researchers tried to interpret data association problem from other aspects. There are two representative works we mainly focus on in this paper. The first one is on basis of energy function [5] which uses standard conjugate gradient optimization and jump-moves methods to find local minimization of a nonconvex optimization. Although this strategy is quite effective as energy function is well-capable in describing the optimal formulation of trajectories through multiple energy terms, yet it will suffer from overwhelming computational cost if the initialization is inappropriate. The other work [6] employs a hierarchical structure [12], which gradually associates the single detection responses into tracklets, and then formulates tracklets into longer trajectories. The key of this method is evaluating and optimizing the affinity on basis of tracklets instead of single detections. Although it can achieve quite efficient performance by calculating the rank of Hankel matrices using fast algorithm, but improper interpolations among targets may arise occasionally because there are no other limitations (such as targets speed) to constrain the linking between two tracklets with similar motion consistency but different IDs.

3   Our Method

In our work, tracking airplanes in ATC surveillance videos is formulated as a problem of tracking multiple homogeneous targets. More specifically, this challenging tracking problem is handled by establishing and minimizing an energy function, wherein most aspects related to the target state are jointly considered. In particular, as the main purpose and strength of the proposed method is to eliminate the possible false associations that may happen near the airport area within the tracking scenes, therefore a novel energy term is deliberately designed and added to the energy function. For constructing this new term to correct wronged associations, priori knowledge is indispensable. The most significant prior information for the problem at hand is the fact that, all airplanes locate within the terminal control area (TMA) should either depart or approach, which means that the starts or ends of trajectories are either in the center or the margin of the scene. Based on this priori knowledge, we hereby introduce the concept of relative distance, which measures the distance from the two endpoints of trajectory to the center of airport respectively. Larger difference value of these two relative distances indicates more probable trajectory.

In practice, trajectories with large relative difference value are set with high confidence scores. Meanwhile, those with smaller value should be punished. Under this premise, the corresponding relative distance energy term is designed, which is the key point to correct the error linking within airport area. In addition, as proper initialization is vital in avoiding additional optimization efforts, we apply Iterating Hankel Total Least Squares (IHTLS) algorithm [6] to generate the initial value and adjust optimization details accordingly, which makes our energy-based framework more effective and efficient.

In Subsect. 3.1, the construction of relative distance difference energy function is elaborated, together with the other energy terms aiming at curing imperfect parts of initial association [6]. In Subsect. 3.2, the details of optimization process, especially two main differences between our method and algorithm proposed in [5] are presented.

3.1 Construction of Energy Function

The energy function implemented in our work takes five different terms:

$$E = c_1 E_{dyn} + c_2 E_{fid} + c_3 E_{res} + c_4 E_{reg} + c_5 E_{exc} \tag{1}$$

where N represents the number of trajectories and F represents the number of frames. Among these five terms, the motion term $E_{dyn}(X) = \sum_{t=1}^{F-2} \sum_{i=1}^{N} ||v_i^t - v_i^{t+1}||^2$, the regularization term $E_{reg} = N$ and the mutual exclusion term $E_{exc} = (\sum_{t=1}^{F} \sum_{i \neq j} \frac{1}{||x_i^t - x_j^t||})/(\sum_{t=1}^{F} N_t)$ are close to the definition in [5]. So we hereby mainly introduce the other two terms E_{fid} and E_{res}.

Fidelity

$$E_{fid} = \theta \sum_{i=1}^{N} \sum_{k} |G_k|^2 + \gamma \sum_{t=1}^{F} (D_t - U_t) \tag{2}$$

Fidelity represents the congruence between trajectories and detections. The first term represents the total number of frames where trajectories do not associate real detection responses but interpolate fake ones, G_k is the length of tracklets without detection responses. The second term represents the number of detections which do not belong to any trajectory, where D_t is the number of detections in frame t and U_t is the part of belonging to trajectories. Although tracking algorithm should have the ability to maintain latent tracklets without detection responses for a certain length, yet the over interpolations operation in algorithm [6] will likely generate fake but not latent tracklets. The fidelity term is therefore designed to punish this situation.

Relative Distance Difference

$$E_{res} = \sum_{i=1}^{N} \frac{1}{|r_s - r_e + 1|} \tag{3}$$

This term is designed to cope with the situation where targets could enter or leave from the center of the scene, which is the main difficulty for realizing reliable MOT in ATC surveillance videos. As the airplanes appearing in the scene always need to take off or land within the airport terminal area that locates at the center of the scene, therefore all trajectories should either start or terminate at the center of the scene, and no aircrafts could travel across the scene. Basing on this prior knowledge, we design the energy term E_{res} to constrain relative distance difference. As shown in formula (3), r_s indicates the distance from the start point of a trajectory to the center of the scene, meanwhile r_e is the distance from end point of that trajectory to the center. According to the prior information elaborated as above, for a correct trajectory, one of the r_s and r_e should be nearly zero while the other one should be large. As a result, the relative distance difference $|r_s - r_e|$ should have a large value for a true trajectory.

3.2   Framework Details

The whole tracking procedure is shown in Fig. 2. The differences between our algorithm and [5] are mainly two-fold: Firstly, we abrogate the conjugate gradient method which was applied in [5] to minimize the continuous energy function. This is because the targets in ATC surveillance videos are so small and the location of detections does not need to be smoothed by optimizing continuous energy minimization; Secondly, we abolish the step of Add operation and execute the step of Split in an iteration, which aims to cope with over-association of initial value.

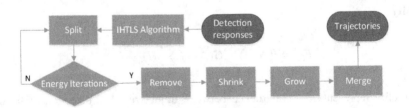

Fig. 2. The framework of our approach

In this paper, we take five fixed-order optimization steps, which include split, remove, shrink, grow and merge. The details of them are shown as follows.

Split and Remove

The purpose of this step is disconnecting obvious wrong associations caused by IHTLS algorithm [6]. Split operation will stop when the value of energy function cannot be lower after energy iterations. In order to avoid disconnecting correct links and obtaining too many fragments, we limit the maximum iterations as i_max.

After the split operation, we need to remove those questionable tracklets without sufficient support from detections. In application, we test the tracklets one by one and remove those that may lower the energy.

Shrink, Grow, Merge

The steps of shrink, grow and merge are similar to [5], in consideration of the length of the article, hereby we would not elaborate on them.

4 Experiment

To testify the effectiveness of the algorithm, we perform experiments on our ATC surveillance videos dataset and the details are illustrated in this section.

4.1 Implementation Details and Parameter Setting

Datasets. In this paper, we conduct the experiments on three available ATC surveillance videos and quantitatively evaluate the tracking results. These videos are screen recordings of radar control machine during actual control process in Tianjin TMA, China. The resolution of images is 2560*1600 and at every frame there are 10 to 15 objects appearing in the scene. Every surveillance video sequence originally lasts about 45 min, and contains 55000 frames with a frame rate of 20 fps. Because radar system can only detect the airplanes in the whole airport terminal area every four seconds, we sample the sequences at an interval of 80 frames to get about 700 valid frames for each.

Detection. In our video, targets may demonstrate four different colors: white, orange, blue and green. As the color of targets in the videos randomly changes during moving, we should design a multi-color template to detect any possible targets. In order to test the robustness of our energy-based association framework, several detection sets with different recall and precision generated by different detector thresholds are prepared for testing.

Parameter Setting. We set all parameters of our method as follows:

1. $[c_1 \ c_2 \ c_3 \ c_4 \ c_5] = [0.05 \ 1 \ 1000 \ 1 \ 136]$
2. $\theta = 1$ and $\gamma = 10$
3. $i\_max = 10$

Evaluation Metrics. For the quantitative evaluation, we adopt the widely used CLEAR MOT metrics [13]. In our sequences, the targets are so small that it is unnecessary to evaluate the tracking precision. In other words, we only calculate the Multi-Object Tracking Accuracy (MOTA) as formula (4) shows, which takes into account three typical errors, false negatives (fn), false positives (fp) and miss match (mm).

$$MOTA = 1 - \frac{\sum_t (fp_t + fn_t + mm_t)}{\sum_t g_t} \qquad (4)$$

4.2   Effectiveness of the Energy-Based Framework

In this section we would first show the effectiveness of energy function integrating with the relative distance difference term E_{res}, which is the main propose of our work. As Fig. 3(a) shows, the No. 6 target lands and goes on takeoff, which is obviously unlikely to happen. We correct this to two different targets land and takeoff in turn shown in Fig. 3(b).

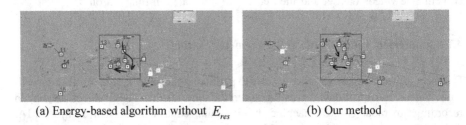

(a) Energy-based algorithm without E_{res} (b) Our method

Fig. 3. Effectiveness of energy function integrating the relative distance difference term.

Table 1 shows the effectiveness of five energy optimization steps. We set the detection threshold as 12.

Table 1. The effectiveness of five energy optimization steps.

Operation	Input	Split	Remove	Shrink	Grow	Merge
Energy	19809.87	19440.92	16567.86	15272.22	15254.32	15251.43
MOTA	0.9578	0.9585	0.9679	0.9737	0.974	0.9742

4.3   Quantitative Comparisons and Qualitative Results

In this section, we first present the quantitative results compared with energy minimization framework [5] and IHTLS algorithm [6] (as shown in Fig. 4) to further verify the effectiveness of our method. As we take the detections under different thresholds as the input of both algorithms, the robustness of our algorithm for different kinds of detection errors is tested as well.

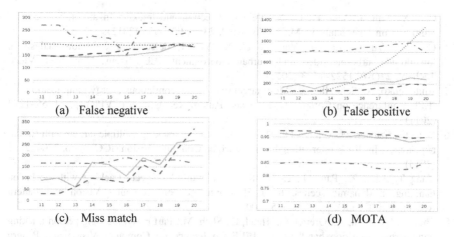

Fig. 4. The red dotted lines denote the detection results. The green dashed lines denote the results of energy minimization algorithm [5]. The yellow solid lines denote the results of IHTLS algorithm [6]. The blue dashed lines denote the results of our method. (Color figure online)

5 Conclusion

In this paper, we design and apply a Multi-object tracking (MOT) algorithm within the ATC surveillance videos to help keep tracks of aircrafts in the terminal area. To solve such a special visual tracking problem where targets demonstrate highly homogenous appearance, a novel TBD-based strategy is proposed which is an integration and modification of two representative tracking algorithms. This strategy solves the tracking under the framework of energy function optimization, where the result of fast association algorithm for similar appearance targets tracking is deployed as the initial value for the optimization. The proposed method is not only suitable for solving our special MOT problem effectively, but also provides a valuable idea for solving other similar special tracking problems. Experiments demonstrate that the proposed formulation performs well when tracking targets within ATC surveillance videos.

Acknowledgement. This paper is supported by the National Science Fund for Distinguished Young Scholars (Grant No. 61425014), the National Natural Science Foundation of China (Grant No. 91538204) and the Foundation for Innovative Research Groups of the National Natural Science Foundation of China (Grant No. 61521091).

References

1. Cao, X., Gao, C., Lan, J., Yuan, Y., Yan, P.: Ego motion guided particle filter for vehicle tracking in airborne videos. Neurocomputing **124**(12), 168–177 (2014)
2. Cao, X., Shi, Z., Yan, P., Li, X.: Tracking vehicles as groups in airborne videos. Neurocomputing **99**(1), 38–45 (2013)

3. Cao, X., Lan, J., Yan, P., Li, X.: Vehicle detection and tracking in airborne videos by multi-motion layer analysis. Mach. Vis. Appl. **23**(5), 921–935 (2012)

4. Cao, X., Wu, C., Lan, J., Yan, P., Li, X.: Vehicle detection and motion analysis in low-altitude airborne video under urban environment. IEEE Trans. Circ. Syst. Video Technol. **21**(10), 1522–1533 (2011)

5. Andriyenko, A., Schindler, K.: Multi-target tracking by continuous energy minimization. In: IEEE Conference on Computer Vision and Pattern Recognition (CVPR), pp. 1265–1272 (2011)

6. Dicle C., Sznaier, M., Camps, O.: The way they move: tracking multiple targets with similar appearance. In: IEEE International Conference on Computer Vision (ICCV), pp. 2304–2311 (2013)

7. Yang T., Li, S.Z., Pan, Q., Li, J.: Real-time multiple objects tracking with occlusion handling in dynamic scenes. In: IEEE Conference on Computer Vision and Pattern Recognition (CVPR), pp. 970–975 (2005)

8. Shu, G., Dehghan, A., Oreifej, O., Hand, E., Shah, M.: Part-based multiple-person tracking with partial occlusion handling. In: IEEE Conference on Computer Vision and Pattern Recognition (CVPR), pp. 1815–1821 (2012)

9. Li, Z., Li, Y., Nevatia, R.: Global data association for multi-object tracking using network flows. In: IEEE Conference on Computer Vision and Pattern Recognition (CVPR), Anchorage, AK, pp. 1–8 (2008)

10. Berclaz, J., Fleuret, F., Turetken, E., Fua, P.: Multiple object tracking using k-shortest paths optimization. PAMI **33**(9), 1806–1819 (2011)

11. Brendel, W., Amer, M.R., Todorovic, S.: Multi-object tracking as maximum weight independent set. In: IEEE Conference on Computer Vision and Pattern Recognition (CVPR), pp. 1273–1280 (2011)

12. Roshan Zamir, A., Dehghan, A., Shah, M.: GMCP-tracker: global multi-object tracking using generalized minimum clique graphs. In: Fitzgibbon, A., Lazebnik, S., Perona, P., Sato, Y., Schmid, C. (eds.) ECCV 2012. LNCS, vol. 7573, pp. 343–356. Springer, Berlin (2012). doi:10.1007/978-3-642-33709-3_25

13. Bernardin, K., Stiefelhagen, R.: Evaluating multiple object tracking performance: the clear mot metrics. EURASIP J. Image Video Proc. **2008**(1), 1–10 (2008)

Identification, Detection, Recognition

Person Re-identification by Multiple Feature Representations and Metric Learning

Meibin Qi, Jingxian Han[✉], and Jianguo Jiang

School of Computer and Information, Hefei University of Technology,
Hefei 230009, China
jingxhan@163.com

Abstract. Person re-identification is the problem of matching pedestrian images captured from multiple cameras. Feature representation and metric designing are two critical aspects in person re-identification. In this paper, we first propose an effective Convolutional Neural Network and learn it with mixed datasets as a general deep feature extractor. Secondly, we extract the hand-crafted feature of images as a supplement, then we learn the independent distance metrics for deep feature representation and hand-crafted feature representation, respectively. Finally, we validate our method on three challenging person re-identification datasets, experimental results show the effectiveness of our approach, and we achieve the best rank-1 matching rates on all the three datasets compare with the state-of-the-art methods.

1   Introduction

Person re-identification aims to identify whether two pedestrian images observed from disjoint camera views belong to the same person or not, which has great significance in video surveillance systems. Large variations in viewpoint, illumination and body posture across different camera views can cause a great appearance variance, which makes the re-identification still a challenging problem. Typically, methods for re-identification include two vital steps: (1) developing robust feature representations to handle the variations in pedestrian images; (2) designing discriminative distance metrics to measure the similarity between pedestrian images.

Representative feature descriptors include [1–8], which mostly come from color and texture. Gray *et al.* [1] used boosting to select a subset of optimal features composed by texture and color features; Farenzena *et al.* [2]proposed Symmetry-Driven Accumulation of Local Features (SDALF) consisted of both symmetry and asymmetry color and texture information; Zhao *et al.* [3] learned the mid-level filter (Mid-Level) from patch clusters with coherent appearance obtained by pruning hierarchical clustering trees to get view-invariant and discriminative features; SalMatch [5] was proposed to exploit both patch matching and salience matching for person re-identification, and in [7], Local Maximal Occurrence (LOMO) was proposed, which was extracted from the local HSV

© Springer Nature Singapore Pte Ltd. 2016
Z. Zhang and K. Huang (Eds.): IVS 2016, CCIS 664, pp. 83–90, 2016.
DOI: 10.1007/978-981-10-3476-3_10

histograms and SILTP features with sliding windows to make a stable representation against viewpoint changes. However, due to the limitations of hand-crafted feature descriptors, it is hard to extract abstract and intrinsic features of the images, which makes these appearance-based features are highly susceptible and difficult to achieve a balance between discriminative power and robustness.

In recent years, many metric learning approaches have been proposed [5,7,9–14] and achieved remarkable performance for person re-identification. Representative methods include Cross-view Quadratic Discriminant Analysis (XQDA) [7], Large Scale Metric Learning from Equivalence Constraint (KISSME) [9], Metric learning to Rank (MLR) [10], Pairwise Constrained Component Analysis (PCCA) [11] and Large Margin Nearest Neighbor (LMNN) [14]. These methods extracted the hand-crafted features first to learn the transformation matrix of the initial feature space, which makes the distance become smaller between the same individuals and larger between different individuals in transformed feature space, some of them achieved impressive improvements for person re-identification.

Compared with the hand-crafted features based methods aforementioned, there are several deep learning based methods have been proposed [15–19]. More abstract and internal features can be learned automatically with the deep architecture, which makes the feature representation rather robust compared with those hand-crafted features. Li *et al.* [15] proposed a novel filter pairing neural network (FPNN) to jointly optimize feature learning, geometric transforms, photometric transforms, misalignment, occlusions and classification. Yi *et al.* [16] used a siamese deep convolutional architecture to learn the texture feature, color feature and metric together in fully cross dataset setting. Ahmed *et al.* [17] presented a deep neural network with layers specially designed for capturing relationships between different camera views. Wu *et al.* [18] used very small convolution filters and increased the depth of the network to improve the performance of re-identification. Xiao *et al.* [19] learned deep feature representation from multiple domains with Convolutional Neural Networks (CNNs). However, these deep neural network need to learn a large number of parameters, small datasets usually can not get remarkable results.

To address these problems, firstly, we learn a general Convolutional Neural Network with the mixture of various datasets as our deep feature extractor, which increases the scale of training set to make small datasets are applicable and enables us learn better features from multiple datasets. Then we extract the appearance-based features of pedestrian images as a supplement. Finally, we learn different metrics for the deep feature representation and hand-crafted feature representation, respectively, which makes the distance metrics more discriminative. Experiments show the superior performance of our proposed approach when compared with the state-of-the-art works.

2   Proposed Approach

In this paper, we extract both deep features and hand-crafted features to represent pedestrian images, and then learn the distance metrics respectively for the two types of feature representations to measure the similarity between different images in a more discriminative way. Section 2.1 introduces the Convolutional Neural Network we proposed to extract the deep feature representation of the images. Section 2.2 introduces the multiple feature representations and our independent metric learning.

2.1 Our Deep Architecture

Inspired by [19,20], we build a CNN model described in Table 1, and mix the various datasets together to train a general CNN as our deep feature extractor for all the datasets. Specifically, three benchmark datasets include VIPER, CUHK01 and CUHK03 are used to validate our method, and all the images are scaled to 144×56 pixels.

Table 1. The Architecture of Our Proposed CNN

Name	Patch size/stride	Input size
conv1	$3 \times 3/1$	$144 \times 56 \times 3$
conv2-conv3	$3 \times 3/1$	$144 \times 56 \times 32$
pool3	$2 \times 2/2$	$144 \times 56 \times 32$
Inception 4a,4b	As in Fig. 1(a)	$78 \times 28 \times 32$
Inception 5a,5b	As in Fig. 1(a)	$36 \times 14 \times 384$
Inception 6a,6b	As in Fig. 1(b)	$18 \times 7 \times 786$
Global pool	$9 \times 4/1$	$9 \times 4 \times 1536$
fc7	Logits	$1 \times 1 \times 1536$
fc8	Logits	$1 \times 4 \times 2048$
Softmax	Classifier	$9 \times 4 \times 2168$

The structure of our CNN is the same with [19] expect the last two Inception modules and the two fully connected layers. Figure 1(b) shows the structure of our last two Inception modules, which was applied to image classification in [20], it expanded the filter bank outputs of the original Inception modules in Fig. 1(a) to promote high dimensional representation. After this, two fully connected layers were applied, the first has 2048 channels and the second contains the channels are equaled with the number of the individuals in training set which is set to 2168 in our model.

2.2 Multi-features Fusion and Independent Metric Learning

After trained the proposed CNN, we extract the fc7 layers output as the deep feature representation for the training and testing set, and exploit the hand-crafted feature LOMO [7] consisted of local HSV histograms and SILTP features

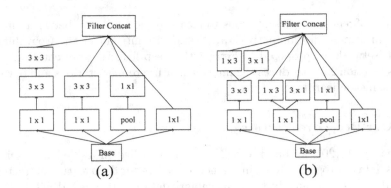

Fig. 1. Inception modules used in our CNN structure, which were all proposed in [20] for image classification, module in (b) is an expanding of (a) to promote high dimensional representations on the coarsest grid

as a complement. Then we learn the independent distance metric with XQDA [7] for the two types of feature representations, respectively.

The XQDA aims to learn a discriminant subspace and an effective distance metric at the same time. Given a pair of images (i, j) captured from different views, $\mathbf{x}_i$ and $\mathbf{y}_j$ are the original features of the images. The distance between image i and j is formulated as:

$$f(\mathbf{x}_i, \mathbf{y}_j) = (\mathbf{x}_i - \mathbf{y}_j)^{\mathrm{T}} \mathbf{W} \mathbf{M} \mathbf{W}^{\mathrm{T}} (\mathbf{x}_i - \mathbf{y}_j) . \tag{1}$$

where $\mathbf{W} \in \mathbb{R}^{d \times r}$ is the subspace projection matrix, $\mathbf{M} \in \mathbb{R}^{r \times r}$ is the learned metric kernel, d is the dimension of the original feature space, and $r(r < d)$ is the dimension of the transformed feature space.

In this paper, we suppose $\mathbf{x}_i^{dr}$ and $\mathbf{x}_i^{hr}$ are the deep feature representation and hand-crafted feature representation of image i, respectively, $\mathbf{y}_j^{dr}$ and $\mathbf{y}_j^{hr}$ have the similar meanings. The distance between image i and j can be re-formulated as:

$$d(i, j) = d_n(\mathbf{x}_i^{dr}, \mathbf{y}_j^{dr}) + d_n(\mathbf{x}_i^{hr}, \mathbf{y}_j^{hr}) . \tag{2}$$

where $d_n(\mathbf{x}_i^{dr}, \mathbf{y}_j^{dr})$ is the normalization of $d(\mathbf{x}_i^{dr}, \mathbf{y}_j^{dr})$, $d_n(\mathbf{x}_i^{hr}, \mathbf{y}_j^{hr})$ is the normalization of $d(\mathbf{x}_i^{hr}, \mathbf{y}_j^{hr})$, which are all calculated by Eq. (1).

3   Experiments

3.1   Datasets and Experiment Protocols

We validate the proposed approach on three widely-used person re-identification datasets include VIPER [21], CUHK01 [22], and CUHK03 [15].

VIPER is one of the most challenging dataset for person re-identification, it contains 632 pairs of person images taken from two camera views with various poses, viewpoints and illumination conditions. The CUHK01 dataset is larger in scale than VIPER, it contains 971 persons captured from two disjoint views and each person has two images in each camera view, camera A captured the frontal or back view of the individuals while camera B captured the side views. And the CUHK03 dataset is one of the most largest published person re-identification datasets, it includes five different pairs of camera views with more than 14,000 images of 1467 pedestrians, in addition, both manually cropped pedestrian images and images automatically detected by the pedestrian detector of [23] are all provided, this is a more realistic setting considering misalignment, occlusions, body part missing and detector errors.

We follow the widely adopted experimental protocols for VIPER and CUHK01 datasets, the individuals in these dataset are randomly divided into half for training and the other half for testing. And for CUHK03, we follow the settings in [19,24], using both manually cropped pedestrian images and images automatically detected together and then randomly select 100 individuals for testing, the other 1367 individuals are used for training. We mix the three selected training sets together to train a general CNN which is employed to extract the deep feature representations of images for various datasets, we use Caffe [25] deep learning framework implement our network. And then we exploit the same individuals used for training our CNN in the three datasets to learn distance metrics for different datasets, respectively. The result is evaluated by cumulative matching characteristic (CMC) curve [26], which is also known as rank-n, an estimate of finding the correct match in the top n match. This procedure is repeated 10 times and the average of rank-n is reported for different dataset.

3.2   Evaluations of Proposed Method

In order to validate the effectiveness of the proposed method, here we conduct a series of experiments with different settings to evaluate the effectiveness of our approach, which include: (i) use our proposed method; (ii) replace our CNN with JSTL [19]; (iii) without hand-crafted feature representation; (iv) without our deep feature representation.

Figure 2 shows the rank-$n(n = 1, 5, 10, 20)$ matching rates for different experiments and datasets. Experimental results show the effectiveness of the proposed method, our method achieves the better performance than other compared methods on all the three datasets. The first two experiments validate the effectiveness of our proposed CNN, by expanding filter bank outputs to promote higher dimensional representation, we can achieve a better performance. And the last two experiments validate that the two types of feature representations can complement each other well.

3.3   Comparison with State-of-the-Arts

We compare our approach with the following state-of-the-art methods: Metric Ensembles (Ensembles) [24], mFilter+LADF [3], mFilter [3], LOMO+XQDA [7], FT-JSTL+DGD [19] and JointRe-id [17]. Figure 3 shows the results on VIPER,

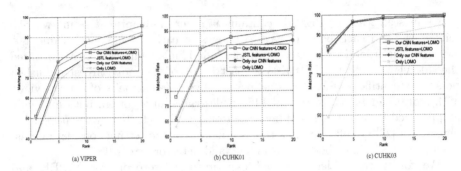

Fig. 2. The experimental results of different methods on the three datasets, measured by rank-1, rank-5, rank-10 and rank-20 matching rates. The red curves represent our proposed method, which achieve the best rank-1 matching rates for all the three datasets (Color figure online)

CUHK01 and CUHK03 datasets. Our method improves rank-1 recognition rates by 5.4%, 7.6% and 8.7% on the three datasets compare with the state-of-the-arts.

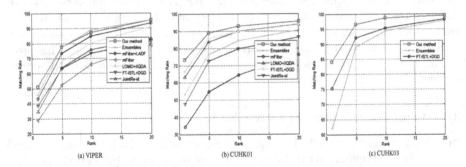

Fig. 3. Performance comparison of the proposed method with the state-of-the-arts for VIPER, CUHK01 and CUHK03 datasets. Our approach outperforms all the state-of-the-art methods in most cases, especially on rank-1 matching rate

4   Conclusion

In this paper, we present an effective deep architecture trained with a mixture of various datasets to extract deep features of pedestrian images, then we use the deep feature representation and hand-crafted feature representation to learn different metrics, respectively. By using both deep feature representation and hand-crafted feature representation, we can gain more robust and comprehensive features, and learning independent distance metrics for the two types feature representation can realize a higher discriminative power. We conduct extensive experiments on three widely used person re-identification datasets to validate our approach. Experimental results demonstrate that our method achieves a better performance than other state-of-the-art methods in most cases.

References

1. Gray, D., Tao, H.: Viewpoint invariant pedestrian recognition with an ensemble of localized features. In: Forsyth, D., Torr, P., Zisserman, A. (eds.) ECCV 2008. LNCS, vol. 5302, pp. 262–275. Springer, Heidelberg (2008). doi:10.1007/978-3-540-88682-2_21

2. Farenzena, M., Bazzani, L., Perina, A., Murino, V., Cristani, M.: Person re-identification by symmetry-driven accumulation of local features. In: Computer Vision and Pattern Recognition (CVPR), vol. 23, pp. 2360–2367 (2010)

3. Zhao, R., Ouyang, W., Wang, X.: Learning mid-level filters for person re-identification. In: CVPR, pp. 144–151 (2014)

4. Hu, Y., Liao, S., Lei, Z., Yi, D., Li, S.Z.: Exploring structural information and fusing multiple features for person re-identification. In: Computer Vision and Pattern Recognition Workshops (CVPRW), vol. 13, pp. 794–799 (2013)

5. Zhao, R., Ouyang, W., Wang, X.: Person re-identification by salience matching. In: Computer Vision (ICCV), pp. 2528–2535 (2013)

6. Ma, B., Su, Y., Jurie, F.: Local descriptors encoded by fisher vectors for person re-identification. In: Fusiello, A., Murino, V., Cucchiara, R. (eds.) ECCV 2012. LNCS, vol. 7583, pp. 413–422. Springer, Heidelberg (2012). doi:10.1007/978-3-642-33863-2_41

7. Liao, S., Hu, Y., Zhu, X., Li, S.Z.: Person re-identification by local maximal occurrence representation and metric learning. In: CVPR, vol. 8, pp. 2197–2206 (2015)

8. Ma, B., Su, Y., Jurie, F.: Covariance descriptor based on bio-inspired features for person re-identification and face verification. Image Vis. Comput. **32**, 379–390 (2014)

9. Koestinger, M., Hirzer, M., Wohlhart, P.: Large scale metric learning from equivalence constraints. In: CVPR, pp. 2288–2295 (2012)

10. McFee, B., Lanckriet, G.R.G.: Metric learning to rank. In: International Conference on Machine Learning, pp. 775–782 (2010)

11. Mignon, A., Jurie, F.: PCCA: a new approach for distance learning from sparse pairwise constraints. In: CVPR, vol. 157, pp. 2666–2672 (2012)

12. Hirzer, M., Roth, P.M., Köstinger, M., Bischof, H.: Relaxed pairwise learned metric for person re-identification. In: Fitzgibbon, A., Lazebnik, S., Perona, P., Sato, Y., Schmid, C. (eds.) ECCV 2012. LNCS, vol. 7577, pp. 780–793. Springer, Heidelberg (2012). doi:10.1007/978-3-642-33783-3_56

13. Zheng, W.S., Gong, S., Xiang, T.: Person re-identification by probabilistic relative distance comparison. In: CVPR, vol. 42, pp. 649–656 (2011)

14. Weinberger, K.Q., Saul, L.K.: Distance metric learning for large margin nearest neighbor classification. J. Mach. Learn. Res. **10**, 207–244 (2009)

15. Li, W., Zhao, R., Xiao, T., Wang, X.: Deepreid: deep filter pairing neural network for person re-identification. In: CVPR, pp. 152–159 (2014)

16. Yi, D., Lei, Z., Li, S.Z.: Deep metric learning for practical person re-identification. In: ICPR, pp. 34–39 (2014)

17. Ahmed, E., Jones, M., Marks, T.K.: An improved deep learning architecture for person re-identification. In: CVPR, pp. 3908–3916 (2015)

18. Wu, L., Shen, C., Hengel, A.V.D.: Personnet: person reidentification with deep convolutional neural networks. arXiv preprint arXiv:1601.07255 (2016)

19. Xiao, T., Li, H., Ouyang, W., Wang, X.: Learning deep feature representations with domain guided dropout for person re-identification. arXiv preprint arXiv:1604.07528 (2016)

20. Szegedy, C., Vanhoucke, V., IoffeSzegedy, S., Shlens, J., Wojna, Z.: Rethinking the inception architecture for computer vision. arXiv preprint arXiv:1512.0056 (2015)

21. Gray, D., Brennan, S., Tao, H.: Evaluating appearance models for recognition, reacquisition, and tracking. In: IEEE International Workshop on Performance Evaluation for Tracking and Surveillance (PETS), vol. 3 (2007)

22. Li, W., Zhao, R., Wang, X.: Human reidentification with transferred metric learning. In: Lee, K.M., Matsushita, Y., Rehg, J.M., Hu, Z. (eds.) ACCV 2012. LNCS, vol. 7724, pp. 31–44. Springer, Heidelberg (2013). doi:10.1007/978-3-642-37331-2_3

23. Felzenszwalb, P.F., Girshick, R.B., McAllester, D., Ramanan, D.: Object detection with discriminatively trained part-based models. Pattern Anal. Mach. Intell. **32**, 1627–1645 (2010)

24. Paisitkriangkrai, S., Shen, C., Hengel, A.V.D.: Learning to rank in person reidentification with metric ensembles. arXiv preprint arXiv:1503.01543 (2015)

25. Jia, Y., Shelhamer, E., Donahue, J., Karayev, S., Long, J., Girshick, R., Guadarrama, S., Darrell, T.: Caffe: convolutional architecture for fast feature embedding. In: ACM, pp. 675–678 (2014)

26. Moon, H., Phillips, P.J.: Evaluating appearance models for recognition, reacquisition, and tracking. Perception **30**, 303–321 (2001)

Deep Multi-level Hashing Codes
for Image Retrieval

Zhenjiang Dong[1,2], Ge Song[3,4], Xia Jia[1], and Xiaoyang Tan[3,4(✉)]

[1] Shanghai Jiaotong University, Shanghai 200240, China
[2] ZTE Corporation, Nanjing 210012, China
[3] Nanjing University of Aeronautics and Astronautics, Nanjing 211106, China
`x.tan@nuaa.edu.cn`
[4] Collaborative Innovation Center of Novel Software Technology
and Industrialization, Nanjing 211106, China

Abstract. In this paper, we propose a deep siamese convolutional neutral network (DSCNN) to learn semantic-preserved global-level and local-level hashing codes simultaneously for effective image retrieval. Particularly, we analyze the visual attention characteristic inside hash bits by activation map of deep convolutional feature and propose a novel approach of bit selecting to reinforce the pertinence of local-level code. Finally, unlike most existing retrieval methods which use global or unsupervised local descriptors separately, leading to unexpected precision, we present a multi-level hash search method, taking advantage of both local and global properties of deep features. The experimental results show that our method outperforms several state-of-the-art on the Oxford 5k/105k and Paris 6k datasets.

1 Introduction

Due to the explosive growth of the Internet, massive images have flooded our daily lives. Image retrieval, i.e. finding images containing the same object or scene as in a query image, has attracted more attention from researchers.

Recently, most studies have reported that deep Convolutional Neural Networks (CNNs) achieved the state of the art performance in many computer vision tasks [1–3]. Notably, many works [4,5] have demonstrated the suitability of features from fully-connected layers for image retrieval. While several works [6–8] focused on features from deep convolutional layers and showed that these features have the natural interpretation as descriptors of local image regions. However, most CNN features for image retrieval are directly extracted from classification model, and subjected to low precision. Furthermore, the features with rich semantic information distract the target sense of query. Early work by Zhou et al. [9] revealed that the convolutional units of CNNs actually behave as object detectors, and proposed a method to generate Class Activation Map (CAM) [10] for localizing the discriminative image regions, which make it available to use deep localizable representations for visual tasks.

© Springer Nature Singapore Pte Ltd. 2016
Z. Zhang and K. Huang (Eds.): IVS 2016, CCIS 664, pp. 91–98, 2016.
DOI: 10.1007/978-981-10-3476-3_11

Besides, traditional nearest neighbor search methods are faced with the computational cost of similarity calculation of high-dimension features, are not appropriate for rapid retrieval, especially under the circumstances of big data age. A practical alternative is to use the hashing based methods [11–13]. Hash method designs a group function which project images into binary codes so that similar images are mapped into similar code. Therefore, the retrieval problem can be done efficiently by computing Hamming distance. Benefiting from deep learning, several researchers [13–17] combined image representations learning with hash learning into one CNN architecture to learn semantic-preserved binary code. Although these methods achieved outstanding performance, have not shed light on the relation between each bit and semantic concept.

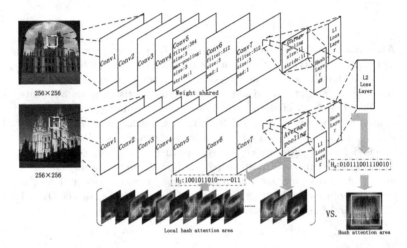

Fig. 1. The DSCNN framework is proposed. Firstly, The semantic-preserved global-level H_g and local-level hash codes H_l are learned. Secondly, we obtain CAMs of each bits of H_g and average these CAMs to acquire 'Hash attention area', and get 'Local hash attention area' by activation maps corresponding to each bits of H_l. Then visually highlight bits (red colored) are selected as compact hash code. Finally, we retrieval similar images by the presented multi-level search strategies. (Color figure online)

In this paper, we propose a deep siamese CNN (DSCNN) framework to learn semantic-preserved hash code, and design the last convolutional layer of DSCNN to obtain local-level hash codes, which is essentially different from other methods [13–15]. Above all, we propose a novel method to obtain compact bits with salient local-semantic. Finally, we present a multi-level hash search method for retrieval.

2   Our Method

Learning Semantic-Preserved Hash Code. It is feasible to embed a latent layer in high-level of a network to output global binary code [13–15]. We follow it and use both label and pair information to guide hash leaning. Otherwise, inspired by discovery [4], we propose to hashing convolutional activations. As Fig. 1 shows, the activation of hash layer and conv7 are both tanh function. And we impose constraints on these layers to embed semantic information. Assuming that the feature maps of conv7 are $\{I_i\}_{i=1}^C \in (-1,1)^{W \times H}$, W, H is weight and height, C is the number of filters, the output of Hash Layer are $a \in (-1,1)^H$, H is the length of hash code. $\hat{y}$ is output of softmax layer, y is expected output. And we minimize the loss function defined following to learn parameters of our network. For local-level hash:

$$L_1 = -\sum_{j=1}^{N} y_i \log(\hat{y}_j) \tag{1}$$

For global-level hash:

$$
\begin{aligned}
L_2 &= -L_1 + \alpha J_{11} + \alpha J_{12} + \beta J_2 + \gamma J_3 \\
&= -\sum_{j=1}^{N} y_i \log(\hat{y}_j) + \alpha \sum_{j=1}^{N} \sum_{i=1}^{N} \delta(y_j = y_i) \|a_j - a_i\|_2^2 \\
&\quad + \alpha \sum_{j=1}^{N} \sum_{i=1}^{N} \delta(y_j \neq y_i) \max(0, c - \|a_j - a_i\|_2^2) \\
&\quad + \beta \sum_{j=1}^{N} (\|\|a_j| - 1\|^2) + \gamma \sum_{j=1}^{N} (\|avg(a_j) - 0\|^2)
\end{aligned}
\tag{2}
$$

where δ is indicator function, avg is the mean function, c is a constant, N is the number of images. The terms L_1 and J_{1*} aim to embed semantic consistency and similarity to hash code respectively. The term J_2 aims to minimize the quantization loss between the learned binary code and the original feature. The last term J_3 enforces evenly distribution of -1 and 1 in hash code. α, β, γ are parameters to balance the effect of different terms.

Finally, the global-level hash code H_g and local-level hash code H_l are defined:

$$H_g = \delta(a > 0), H_l = \delta(f > 0)$$

$$where f \in (-1,1)^C, f_k = \frac{1}{W \times H} \sum_{i=1}^{W} \sum_{j=1}^{H} I_k(i,j) \tag{3}$$

Selecting Compact Bits. The deep convolutional feature maps are activated with different regions [18,19]. And through careful observation we found that some feature maps are not related to the salient area, it may be possible to boost feature discrimination by discarding unrelated feature maps. Therefore we propose to select compact bit to enforce retrieval performance.

The first stage is to catch the attention region of H_g. We compute CAMs of H_g. Then we average these maps to M_{avg} and binarize by $B_{avg} = \delta(M_{avg} > \theta)$, where θ is a threshold. And we get attention region by finding the largest connected subgraph of B_{avg}. As Fig. 1 shows.

The second stage is selecting local feature maps. We convert all feature maps of Conv7 into activation maps $\{AM_i\}_{i=1}^{C}$ by up-sampling, and obtain corresponding binary maps $\{B_i\}_{i=1}^{C}$ as the first stage done. We definite the score of relevant to salient area of feature maps as follows:

$$S(B_i, B_{avg}) = sum(B_i \wedge B_{avg}) \tag{4}$$

where $\wedge$ is AND operation bit-by-bit, sum represents sum all elements of matrix.

In the last stage, Ranking $I_1, I_2, \ldots, I_C$ by their scores S and selecting top L filters as informative local features. Then we choose associated L bits of H_l as $H_l^{'}$ for efficient retrieval. In our experiment, we only compared the local-level hash code of query's L positions with corresponding position bits of others.

$$H_q^{'} = \Psi_q(H_q), d_H(H_q^{'}, H_i) = d_H(H_q^{'}, \Psi_q(H_i)) \tag{5}$$

where $\Psi_q(*)$ indicates obtain the bits of $*$ as the same positions as H_q.

Searching via Multi-level Hashing. The original data space could be mapped to Hamming space by several group hash functions with similarity structure preserved separately. We proposed a multi-level search method of hashing, using several sets of function with different properties to reinforce positive neighborhoods retrieval and develop two strategies.

Rerank-Based Strategy#1. Firstly, we use global-level hash code to retrieval and select top K as candidates. Then, we use local-level hash code to rerank these candidates.

Hamming Distance Weighted Strategy#2. Assuming that query image x_q and N images $\{x_i\}_{i=1}^{N}$ and corresponding global-level hash code $H_{gq}, \{H_{gi}\}_{i=1}^{N}$ and local-hash code $H_{lq}^{'}, \{H_{li}\}_{i=1}^{N}$. Fusing distance as:

$$Sim(x_q, x_i) = \lambda d_H(H_{gq}, H_{gi}) + (1 - \lambda)d_H(H_{lq}^{'}, H_{li}) \tag{6}$$

In experiments, we firstly retrieval use the global-level code, then rerank by proposed weighted strategy.

3   Experiments

Datasets. We evaluate performance on three standard datasets with mean average precision (MAP). Oxford Buildings [20] (Oxford5k) contains 5063 images, including 55 queries corresponding 11 landmark buildings. Oxford Buildings+100K [20] (Oxford105k) includes Oxford5k and extra 100K images as distractor. Paris Buildings [21] (Paris6k) contains 6412 images, 55 queries corresponding to 11 Paris landmarks.

Experimental Details. We implement the proposed DSCNN by Caffe [22] package. We design DSCNN based on the AlexNet architecture, details as

Fig. 1 shows. All images are resized to 256×256 before passing through the network. For training model, we randomly select positive and negative pairs from dataset exclude queries and initial weights of Conv1-Conv4 with pre-trained AlexNet.

Fig. 2. Examples of the compact of using local-level code to reranking. For each query image, the first line represents the rankings with global-level hash code, and the next line is the retrieval result by using proposed multi-level hash search method.

Results of Local Features. We compare local-level code from DSCNN with other state local descriptors. Firstly, we compare with the sophisticated local descriptors aggregation methods Fisher vectors [6], VLAD [23] and Tri. embedding [24]. Table 1 summaries the results. We attain the best performance on three datasets. Compared with deep feature, we can see that our average-pooling strategy (local-level hash) outperforms max-pooling [25] and SPoC [6] on Oxford dataset. Then, the result on Paris demonstrates that the local-level is superior to global-level hash code. And multi-level improve the performance of global-level code by 12 and 14 on Oxford and Paris, respectively. Some qualitative examples of retrieval using multi-level hash are shown in Fig. 2, local-level hash enhances the ranking of relevant results and decrease the irrelevant images, as expected. Finally, our method is different from PCA and performs better.

Table 1. mAP comparison with local descriptors. Local-level hash perform better.

Method	D	Oxford5k	Oxford105k	Paris6k
Fisher Vector [6]	256	54.0	-	-
Trian. embedding [24]	1024	56.0	50.2	-
VLAD [6]	128	44.8	37.4	55.5
CNN+VLAD [8]	128	55.8	-	58.3
CNN+Max pooling [25]	256	53.3	48.9	67.0
SPoC [6]	256	58.9	57.8	-
Conv7+PCA	256	58.6	55.7	68.6
global-level hash code	48	59.3	58.2	69.2
local-level hash code	256	**69.7**	**63.9**	**85.2**
multi-level hash code	256	67.1	63.4	83.7

Comparison with State-of-the-Art. Approaches based on deep model in the literature. We set length of H_l to 256 impartially. As Table 2 reveals that our method produced better or competitive results. For strategy #1, we use global-level hash code to retrieval 50 candidates and rerank by local-level hash code, achieving mAP 67.1% on Oxford5k and 83.7% on Paris6k. Then, we adopt strategy #2 to retrieval with setting λ to 0.5 empirically, obtaining slightly different performance with strategy#1. We conjectured that the fusion weaken some discriminant of local-level code caused the gap in performance.

For deep convolutional features, CNN+fine-tuning [26] gains mAP 55.7% on Oxford by retraining deep models with additional landmarks dataset collected by themselves, while we obtain 67.2% only with limited training samples provide by datasets. Although we did not promote performance by spatial reranking or query expansion strategies as Tolias et al. [7] done, our method achieve competitive results. Compared with R-CNN+CS-SR+QE [26], our method is more simple and effective (83.7 vs 78.4), exploring the inside property of deep convolutional descriptor to select compact local feature for retrieval, while R-CNN+CS-SR+QE locates objects by RPN. Mention that our method can carry out fast image retrieval via Hamming distance measurement, which is obviously superior to others based on Euclidean or Cosine distance.

Table 2. mAP comparison with state-of-the-art methods CNN-based.

Method	Oxford5k	Oxford105k	Paris6k
SPoC [6]	58.9	57.8	-
Razavian et al. [5]	55.6	-	69.7
Kalantidis et al. [27]	65.4	59.3	77.9
Tolias et al. [7]	66.8	61.6	83.0
CNN+fine-tuning et al. [4]	55.7	52.4	-
R-CNN+CS-SR+QE [26]	**67.8**	-	78.4
Ours(#1)	67.1	**63.4**	**83.7**
Ours(#2)	67.2	62.8	83.4

4 Conclusion

This paper has presented a deep siamese CNN to produce global and local levels hash codes for image retrieval with the proposed multi-level search method. And we firstly propose to select region-related bits by activation maps. Finally, we demonstrate the efficacy and applicability of the proposed approach on retrieval benchmarks. Experimental results show that our method improves the previous performance on Oxford and Paris datasets, respectively.

Acknowledgements. This work is supported by National Science Foundation of China (61373060,61672280), Qing Lan Project and the Research Foundation of ZTE Corporation.

References

1. Krizhevsky, A., Sutskever, I., Hinton, G.E.: Imagenet classification with deep convolutional neural networks. In: Advances in Neural Information Processing Systems, vol. 2012 (2012)
2. Szegedy, C., Toshev, A., Erhan, D.: Deep neural networks for object detection. In: Advances in Neural Information Processing Systems, pp. 2553–2561 (2013)
3. Long, J., Shelhamer, E., Darrell, T.: Fully convolutional networks for semantic segmentation. Computer Science, pp. 1337–1342 (2015)
4. Babenko, A., Slesarev, A., Chigorin, A., Lempitsky, V.: Neural codes for image retrieval. In: Fleet, D., Pajdla, T., Schiele, B., Tuytelaars, T. (eds.) ECCV 2014. LNCS, vol. 8689, pp. 584–599. Springer, Heidelberg (2014). doi:10.1007/978-3-319-10590-1_38
5. Razavian, A.S., Azizpour, H., Sullivan, J., Carlsson, S.: CNN features off-the-shelf: an astounding baseline for recognition. In: IEEE Conference on Computer Vision and Pattern Recognition Workshops, pp. 512–519 (2014)
6. Babenko, A., Lempitsky, V.: Aggregating deep convolutional features for image retrieval. Computer Science (2015)
7. Tolias, G., Sicre, R., Jgou, H.: Particular object retrieval with integral max-pooling of CNN activations. Computer Science (2015)
8. Ng, Y.H., Yang, F.: Davis, L.S.: Exploiting local features from deep networks for image retrieval. Computer Science, pp. 53–61 (2015)
9. Zhou, B., Khosla, A., Lapedriza, A., Oliva, A., Torralba, A.: Object detectors emerge in deep scene CNNs. Computer Science (2014)
10. Zhou, B., Khosla, A., Lapedriza, A., Oliva, A., Torralba, A.: Learning deep features for discriminative localization. Computer Science (2015)
11. Andoni, A., Indyk, P.: Near-optimal hashing algorithms for approximate nearest neighbor in high dimensions. In: Annual Symposium on Foundations of Computer Science, pp. 117–122 (2006)
12. Liong, V.E., Lu, J., Wang, G., Moulin, P., Zhou, J.: Deep hashing for compact binary codes learning. In: Computer Vision and Pattern Recognition (2015)
13. Zhao, F., Huang, Y., Wang, L., Tan, T.: Deep semantic ranking based hashing for multi-label image retrieval. In: Computer Vision and Pattern Recognition (2015)
14. Lin, K., Yang, H.F., Hsiao, J.H., Chen, C.S.: Deep learning of binary hash codes for fast image retrieval. In: Computer Vision and Pattern Recognition Workshops, pp. 27–35 (2015)
15. Li, W.J., Wang, S., Kang, W.C.: Feature learning based deep supervised hashing with pairwise labels. Computer Science (2015)
16. Lai, H., Pan, Y., Liu, Y., Yan, S.: Simultaneous feature learning and hash coding with deep neural networks. In: Computer Vision and Pattern Recognition (2015)
17. Liu, H., Wang, R., Shan, S., Chen, X.: Deep supervised hashing for fast image retrieval. In: Computer Vision and Pattern Recognition (2016)
18. Zeiler, M.D., Fergus, R.: Visualizing and understanding convolutional networks. In: Fleet, D., Pajdla, T., Schiele, B., Tuytelaars, T. (eds.) ECCV 2014. LNCS, vol. 8689, pp. 818–833. Springer, Heidelberg (2014). doi:10.1007/978-3-319-10590-1_53

19. Mahendran, A., Vedaldi, A.: Understanding deep image representations by inverting them. In: Computer Vision and Pattern Recognition (2015)
20. Philbin, J., Chum, O., Isard, M., Sivic, J.: Object retrieval with large vocabularies and fast spatial matching. In: Computer Vision and Pattern Recognition (2007)
21. Philbin, J., Chum, O., Isard, M., Sivic, J., Zisserman, A.: Lost in quantization: improving particular object retrieval in large scale image databases. In: Computer Vision and Pattern Recognition (2008)
22. Jia, Y., Shelhamer, E., Donahue, J., Karayev, S., Long, J., Girshick, R., Guadarrama, S., Darrell, T.: Caffe: convolutional architecture for fast feature embedding. Eprint Arxiv, pp. 675–678 (2014)
23. Arandjelovic, R., Zisserman, A.: All about VLAD. In: IEEE Conference on Computer Vision and Pattern Recognition, pp. 1578–1585 (2013)
24. Jegou, H., Zisserman, A.: Triangulation embedding and democratic aggregation for image search. In: Computer Vision and Pattern Recognition, pp. 3310–3317 (2014)
25. Razavian, A.S., Sullivan, J., Maki, A., Carlsson, S.: A baseline for visual instance retrieval with deep convolutional networks. Computer Science (2015)
26. Salvador, A., Giro-I-Nieto, X., Marques, F., Satoh, S.: Faster R-CNN features for instance search. Eprint Arxiv (2016)
27. Kalantidis, Y., Mellina, C., Osindero, S.: Cross-dimensional weighting for aggregated deep convolutional features. Eprint Arxiv (2015)

Salient Object Detection from Single Haze Images via Dark Channel Prior and Region Covariance Descriptor

Nan Mu[1], Xin Xu[1,2(✉)], and Xiaolong Zhang[1,2]

[1] School of Computer Science and Technology, Wuhan University of Science and Technology, Wuhan, China
xuxin0336@163.com
[2] Hubei Province Key Laboratory of Intelligent Information Processing and Real-time Industrial System, Wuhan University of Science and Technology, Wuhan, China

Abstract. Due to degraded visibility and low contrast, object detection from single haze images faces great challenges. This paper proposed to use a computational model of visual saliency to cope with this issue. Superpixel-level saliency map is firstly abstracted via the dark channel prior. Then, region covariance descriptors are utilized to estimate local and global saliency of each superpixel. Besides, the graph model is incorporated as constraint to optimize the correlation between superpixels. Experimental results verify the validity and efficiency of the proposed saliency computational model.

Keywords: Single haze image · Saliency · Covariance · Dark channel · Superpixel

1 Introduction

According to the statistical reports from the ministry of public security, more than 10% of the road traffic accidents are directly related to bad weather, such as fog and haze, the visibility is significantly degraded in these scenes. Optically, the reason is due to the floating particles in the air, which absorb and scatter much light.

To address this issue, a plethora of defogging algorithms have been developed in recent decades. By utilizing image dehazing technology, the color and visibility of the single haze image can be restored to some degree. Although the dehazing processing can increase the identification of salient region substantially, the background information is also enhanced. As a result, the real salient object of the defogging image can not be detected correctly by the state-of-the-art saliency models (e.g. Fig. 1).

Typically, haze images have low contrast and low resolution, which cause the visual features difficult to extract. Thus, saliency detection in haze image faces several problems: (1) For most features become invalid in low visibility conditions, the accuracy of detection result can't be ensured by traditional feature extraction methods. (2) Due to lack of edge and contour information, there has little difference between foreground and background in haze image, it makes salient object hardly distinguished.

© Springer Nature Singapore Pte Ltd. 2016
Z. Zhang and K. Huang (Eds.): IVS 2016, CCIS 664, pp. 99–106, 2016.
DOI: 10.1007/978-981-10-3476-3_12

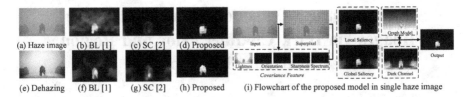

(a) Haze image   (b) BL [1]   (c) SC [2]   (d) Proposed   Input   Superpixel   Local Saliency   Graph Model

Output

Lightnes   Orientation   Sharpness Spectrum
Covariance Feature

(e) Dehazing   (f) BL [1]   (g) SC [2]   (h) Proposed   (i) Flowchart of the proposed model in single haze image   Global Saliency   Dark Channel

Fig. 1. Saliency maps comparison between haze image (a) and the pre-processing image (e).

Conventional saliency methods had mainly followed Itti's model [3], which based on the multi-scale features and center-surrounded contrast. According to the perceptual mechanism of *human visual system* (HVS), contrast plays a key role in visual saliency computation. Current models estimate the saliency of each image region by computing the contrast from local or global perspective.

Local methods compute saliency between each image region and its local neighborhood. Rigas *et al.* [4] constructed saliency map by extracting image features via local sparse coding. Nouri *et al.* [5] modeled the mesh saliency by using local adaptive patches. Such models tend to highlight salient objects near edges instead of the whole regions. Global methods estimate saliency between each region and the whole image. Our previous model [6] computed saliency by global contrast measure and color distribution. Zhang *et al.* [7] proposed a nonlocal anisotropic diffusion equation based saliency model. These global models can get a uniform saliency region.

In this paper, we employ both local and global estimation to define the saliency of each superpixel. For the accuracy of salient object detection is directly affected by the feature extraction, which is the main step to turn the visual stimuli into visual information for processing. The saliency of each superpixel is computed the by two descriptors including dark channel and covariance feature, which can better eliminate the influence of the haze background. To optimize the saliency map, a graph model is exploited to enhance the visual effect. Experimental results on the haze image dataset demonstrate that the generated saliency map has favorable performance in comparing with nine state-of-the-art saliency models.

2 Proposed Salient Object Detection Model

2.1 Superpixel Based Graph Construction

The proposed method creates superpixels by using *simple linear iterative clustering* (SLIC) algorithm [8]. The input image is first divided the into superpixels $SP(i)$, where $i = 1, \cdots, N$ and $N = 300$ is sufficient to guarantee a good boundary recall.

After superpixel segmentation, a graph $G = (v, e)$ of N nodes is constructed to represent the input image, where v is the nodes set and each node corresponds to a superpixel; e is the edges set and is weighted by an affinity matrix $A_m = [a_{ij}]N \times N$. Given the graph G and the saliency seeds $s = [s_1, s_2, \cdots, s_N]^T$, the diffusion process spreads the seeds s through graph G based on the optimal affinity matrix. The saliency diffusions $S^* = [S_1^*, S_2^*, \cdots, S_N^*]^T$ of each node are calculated via: $S^* = D_m \cdot s$, where D_m denotes the diffusion matrix, which is equal to $(I_m - \beta \cdot L_m)^{-1}$ in (1).

The goal of manifold ranking is to compute a rank for each node in graph. By utilizing the manifold ranking through graph G, the similarity between superpixels can be described more accuracy. Given G, as in [9], the ranking function is defined by:

$$S^* = (I_m - \beta \cdot L_m)^{-1} s, \qquad (1)$$

where I_m is the identity matrix of G, parameter β controls the balance of unary and pairwise potentials in manifold ranking, and L_m is the normalized Laplacian matrix.

2.2   Dark Channel Based Depth Information Extraction

The dark channel prior is proposed to remove the haze from input image in [10]. According to the observation of outdoor images, some pixels or regions usually have at least one color channel, which has very low intensity. It means that the dark channel of image pixels is mainly generated by the dark regions, which usually appear in the salient objects. For a pixel $I(x, y)$, the dark channel prior is defined as:

$$I_{dark}(x, y) = 1 - \min_{c \in \{R,G,B\}} \left(\min_{x,y \in p(x,y)} (I^c(x, y)) \right), \qquad (2)$$

where I^c is a color channel of image I and $p(x, y)$ is a local patch centered around $I(x, y)$. Then, the dark channel prior of each superpixel $SP(i)$ is computed by:

$$I_{dark}(SP(i)) = \frac{1}{num(SP(i))} \sum_{x,y \in SP(i)} I_{dark}(x, y), \qquad (3)$$

where $num(SP(i))$ is number of pixels within the superpixel $SP(i)$.

The low intensity region in haze image can be effective recognized by the dark channel computation. Thus, the dark regions, colorful surfaces or the specific objects are picked out from haze image. These factors are also components of salient objects.

2.3   Feature Based Region Covariance

The proposed model uses covariance matrices of superpixels as meta-features for saliency estimation. The structure information can be better captured by region covariance, which can also integrate features in a nonlinearly way. In our work, several visual features are extracted, namely lightness, orientation, sharpness, and spectrum.

Lightness Feature: The lightness feature (denoted as $L(x, y)$) is got from the light channel in Lab color space, although the color information would fade in haze images, the glow amount of an image is still an important indicator to measure object saliency.

Orientation Feature: For an input image I, the horizontal gradient (denoted as $|\partial I/\partial x|$) and the vertical gradient (denoted as $|\partial I/\partial y|$) are the norm of first order derivatives of the intensity image, which can represent the edge orientation information. The distribution and difference of the brightness in the haze scenes can be highlighted by the gradient amplitude.

Sharpness Feature: Sharpness is proportional to the variations of image grayscale and texture complication between a pixel and its neighbor pixels. The sharpness feature (denoted as $Shar(x,y)$) is computed by the convolution of grayscale image and the first-order derivatives of the Gaussian in vertical and horizontal directions [11].

Spectrum Feature: The spectrum feature (denoted as $Spec(x,y)$) is measured by the difference between log spectrum and amplitude [12], which is less affected by the image contrast and more robust to noise.

Based on these features, the image is converted into a 5-dimensional feature vector:

$$F(x,y) = \left[L(x,y) \left| \frac{\partial I(x,y)}{\partial x} \right| \left| \frac{\partial I(x,y)}{\partial y} \right| Shar(x,y) Spec(x,y) \right]^{T}. \tag{4}$$

For each superpixel region $SP(i)$ inside F, it can be represented as a 5×5 covariance matrix [13] via:

$$C_i = \frac{1}{n-1} \sum_{i=1}^{n} (f_i(x,y) - \mu^*)(f_i(x,y) - \mu^*)^T, \tag{5}$$

where $\{f_i(x,y)\}_{i=1,\cdots,n}$ denote the 5-dimensional feature points inside $SP(i)$ and μ^* is the mean value of these points.

The multiple features, which might be correlated, can be naturally fused by covariance matrix. The dissimilarity between two covariance matrices is measure by [14]:

$$\rho(C_i, C_j) = \sqrt{\sum_{k=1}^{5} \ln^2 E_k(C_i, C_j)}, \tag{6}$$

where $\{E_k(C_i, C_j)\}_{k=1,\cdots,5}$ are the generalized eigenvalues of C_i and C_j.

2.4   Covariance Based Saliency Estimation

Given an input haze image, the saliency of superpixel region R_i is defined by the weighted average of covariance dissimilarities between R_i and its surrounding region.

For local saliency estimation, the surrounding region of R_i is found according to its affinity matrix. The local saliency of R_i is computes as:

$$s(R_i) = \frac{1}{\lambda_i} \sum_{j=1}^{\lambda_i} d(R_i, R_j), \tag{7}$$

where λ_i is the numbers of adjacent superpixel regions (denoted as $R_j, j = 1, \cdots, \lambda_i$) of R_i, $d(R_i, R_j)$ is the dissimilarity between R_i and R_j, which is given by:

$$d(R_i, R_j) = \frac{\rho(C_i, C_j)}{1 + |c^*(i) - c^*(j)|}, \tag{8}$$

where C_i and C_j denote the covariance matrix of R_i and R_j, $c^*(i)$ and $c^*(j)$ denote the center of R_i and R_j, respectively. For global saliency estimation, we choose the whole image region as the surrounding region of R_i.

2.5 Diffusion-Based Saliency Optimization

After calculating the saliency of all the superpixel regions, a seed vector s is obtained, which contains a saliency value per graph node. Then the diffusion process given by (1) and dark channel prior given by (3) are utilized to optimize the results. The saliency value of superpixel $SP(i)$ is constructed by:

$$S_{saliency}(SP(i)) = D_m \times s(R_i) \times I_{dark}(SP(i)). \tag{9}$$

Finally, two different saliency maps S_{local} and S_{global} are efficiently obtained by the proposed local and global methods, which are complementary to each other. We integrate these two saliency maps by weighted geometric: $S_{map} = S_{local}^{\varepsilon} \times S_{global}^{1-\varepsilon}$, $\varepsilon = 0.5$.

3 Experimental Results

The proposed algorithm is evaluated on the haze image dataset, which contains 200 haze images with the binary ground truths. Our model is compared with nine state-of-the-art saliency models, including *low rank matrix recovery* (LR) model [15], *context-aware* (CA) model [16], *patch distinction* (PD) model [17], *graph-based manifold ranking* (GBMR) model [18], *saliency optimization* (SO) model [19], *cellular automata* (BSCA) model [20], *bootstrap learning* (BL) model [1], *spatiochromatic context* (SC) model [2], and *generic promotion of diffusion-based* (GP) model [21].

The performance evaluation is conducted according to four metrics. The first metric compares the *true positive rates* (TPRs) and the *false positive rates* (FPRs). Figure 2(a)

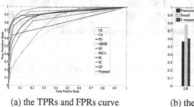

(a) the TPRs and FPRs curve

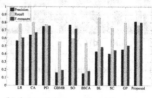

(b) the precision, recall and F-measure

Fig. 2. Quantitative comparisons of the proposed saliency model with nine models.

shows the TPR-FPR curve for comparing the proposed saliency model with the aforementioned nine saliency models.

The second metric compares the precision, recall, F-measure rate. Precision measures the accuracy of the resulting saliency map. Recall measures the completeness of the detected salient objects. F-measure is calculated as the weighted harmonic mean between precision and recall. The quantitative comparisons of various models are shown in Fig. 2(b), it shows that our model significantly outperforms the others.

The third metric compares the AUC (area under the curve) score, which is calculated as the area under the TPR-FPR curve. The perfect saliency model will score close to 1. The forth metric compares the *mean absolute error* (MAE) score, which evaluates the true negative saliency assignment. The MAE score is calculated as the difference between the saliency map and the ground truth. The AUC and MAE scores are listed in Table 1. Obviously, the proposed model achieves a relatively better performance scores on the haze image dataset. The average computation times of ten saliency models are also compared in Table 1, which are measured at a PC machine with an Intel Pentium G2020 2.90 GHz CPU and 12 GB RAM. All these ten models are implemented by using MATLAB.

Table 1. The performance comparisons of various saliency models in haze images

	LR	CA	PD	GBMR	SO	BSCA	BL	SC	GP	Proposed
AUC	0.8919	0.9440	0.9294	0.8047	0.8108	0.7298	0.9138	0.8466	0.8969	0.9747
MAE	0.1375	0.1578	0.1155	0.2889	0.1038	0.2824	0.2451	0.1397	0.2074	0.0964
TIME(s)	73.5214	35.4267	32.6920	1.6726	2.5709	3.1887	91.4533	58.6289	15.9652	9.8337

The visual comparisons of saliency maps obtained by these various saliency models are presented in Fig. 3. As can be intuitively observed from Fig. 3, the saliency maps produced by the proposed model are closest to the ground truth and can deal well with the challenging haze images.

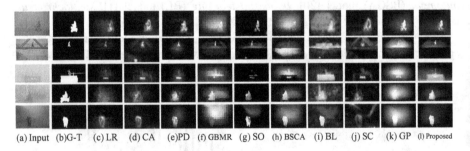

(a) Input (b)G-T (c) LR (d) CA (e)PD (f) GBMR (g) SO (h) BSCA (i) BL (j) SC (k) GP (l) Proposed

Fig. 3. The saliency maps of the proposed model in comparison with nine models.

4 Conclusion

In this paper, we focus on modeling saliency by estimating the local and global contrast of all superpixels, and present a dark channel and covariance feature based saliency model. The dark channel processor can better restrain the impact of haze background. The covariance feature can be robust to deal with the low contrast single haze images. To further improve the visual performance, a diffusion process is employed to enhance the internal relevance of salient object. Extensive experimental results have shown that the proposed saliency model performs favorably against 9 state-of-the-art models on the haze image dataset.

Acknowledgments. This work was supported by the Natural Science Foundation of China (61602349, 61273225, 61273303, and 61403287) and the China Scholarship Council (201508420248).

References

1. Tong, N., Lu, H., Yang, M.: Salient object detection via bootstrap learning. In: Proceedings of IEEE Conference on Computer Vision and Pattern Recognition, pp. 1884–1892 (2015)
2. Zhang, J., Wang, M., Zhang, S., Li, X., Wu, X.: Spatiochromatic context modeling for color saliency analysis. IEEE Trans. Neural Netw. Learn. Syst. 27(6), 1177–1189 (2016)
3. Itti, L., Koch, C., Niebur, E.: A model of saliency-based visual attention for rapid scene analysis. IEEE Trans. Pattern Anal. Mach. Intell. 20(11), 1254–1259 (1998)
4. Rigas, I., Economou, G., Fotopoulos, S.: Efficient modeling of visual saliency based on local sparse representation and the use of hamming distance. Comput. Vis. Image Underst. 134, 33–45 (2015)
5. Nouri, A., Charrier, C., Lezoray, O.: Multi-scale mesh saliency with local adaptive patches for viewpoint selection. Sig. Process. Image Commun. 38, 151–166 (2015)
6. Xu, X., Mu, N., Chen, L., Zhang, X.: Hierarchical salient object detection model using contrast based saliency and color spatial distribution. Multimedia Tools Appl. 75(5), 2667–2679 (2015)
7. Zhang, X., Xu, C., Li, M., Teng, R.K.F.: Study of visual saliency detection via nonlocal anisotropic diffusion equation. Pattern Recogn. 48(4), 1315–1327 (2015)
8. Achanta, R., Shaji, A., Smith, K., Lucchi, A., Fua, P., Susstrunk, S.: SLIC superpixels compared to state-of-the-art superpixel methods. IEEE Trans. Pattern Anal. Mach. Intell. 34 (11), 2274–2282 (2012)
9. Yan, Q., Xu, L., Shi, J., Jia, J.: Hierarchical saliency detection. In: Proceedings of IEEE Conference on Computer Vision and Pattern Recognition, pp. 1155–1162 (2013)
10. He, K., Sun, J., Tang, X.: Single image haze removal using dark channel prior. IEEE Trans. Pattern Anal. Mach. Intell. 33(12), 2341–2353 (2011)
11. Xu, X., Mu, N., Zhang, H., Fu, X.: Salient object detection from distinctive features in low contrast images. In: Proceedings of IEEE International Conference on Image Processing, pp. 3126–3130 (2015)
12. Hou, X., Zhang, L.: Saliency detection: a spectral residual approach. In: Proceedings of IEEE Conference on Computer Vision and Pattern Recognition, pp. 1–8 (2007)

13. Tuzel, O., Porikli, F., Meer, P.: Region covariance: a fast descriptor for detection and classification. In: Leonardis, A., Bischof, H., Pinz, A. (eds.) ECCV 2006. LNCS, vol. 3952, pp. 589–600. Springer, Heidelberg (2006). doi:10.1007/11744047_45

14. Forstner, W., Moonen, B.: A metric for covariance matrices. In: Grafarend, E.W., Krumm, W., Schwarze, V.S. (eds.) Geodesy-The Challenge of the 3rd Millennium, pp. 299–309. Springer, Berlin (2003)

15. Shen, X., Wu, Y.: A unified approach to salient object detection via low rank matrix recovery. In: Proceedings of IEEE Conference on Computer Vision and Pattern Recognition, pp. 853–860 (2012)

16. Goferman, S., Zelnik-Manor, L., Tal, A.: Context-aware saliency detection. Proc. IEEE Trans. Pattern Anal. Mach. Intell. **34**(10), 1915–1926 (2012)

17. Margolin, R., Tal, A., Zelnik-Manor, L.: What makes a patch distinct? In: Proceedings of IEEE Conference on Computer Vision and Pattern Recognition, pp. 1139–1146 (2013)

18. Yang, C., Zhang, L., Lu, H., Ruan, X., Yang, M.-H.: Saliency detection via graph-based manifold ranking. In: Proceedings of IEEE Conference on Computer Vision and Pattern Recognition, pp. 3166–3137 (2013)

19. Zhu, W., Liang, S., Wei, Y., Sun, J.: Saliency optimization from robust background detection. In: Proceedings of IEEE Conference on Computer Vision and Pattern Recognition, pp. 2814–2821 (2014)

20. Qin, Y., Lu, H., Xu, Y., Wang, H.: Saliency detection via cellular automata. In: Proceedings of IEEE Conference on Computer Vision and Pattern Recognition, pp. 110–119 (2015)

21. Jiang, P., Vasconcelos, N., Peng, J.: Generic promotion of diffusion-based salient object detection. In: Proceedings of IEEE International Conference on Computer Vision, pp. 217–225 (2015)

Hybrid Patch Based Diagonal Pattern Geometric Appearance Model for Facial Expression Recognition

Deepak Kumar Jain[1,2,3](✉), Zhang Zhang[1,2,3], and Kaiqi Huang[1,2,3]

[1] Center for Research on Intelligent Perception and Computing,
Institute of Automation, Chinese Academy of Sciences, Beijing, China
deepak.juet@cripac.ia.ac.cn
[2] National Laboratory of Pattern Recognition, Institute of Automation,
Chinese Academy of Sciences, Beijing, China
[3] University of Chinese Academy of Sciences, Beijing, China

Abstract. Automatic Facial Expression Recognition (FER) is an imperative process in next generation Human-Machine Interaction (HMI) for clinical applications. The detailed information analysis and maximization of labeled database are the major concerns in FER approaches. This paper proposes a novel Patch-Based Diagonal Pattern (PBDP) method on Geometric Appearance Models (GAM) that extracts the features in a multi-direction for detailed information analysis. Besides, this paper adopts the co-training to learn the complementary information from RGB-D images. Finally, the Relevance Vector Machine (RVM) classifier is used to recognize the facial expression. In experiments, we validate the proposed methods on two RGB-D facial expression datasets, i.e., EURECOMM dataset and biographer dataset. Compared to other methods, the comparative analysis regarding the recognition and error rate prove the effectiveness of the proposed PBDP-GAM in FER applications.

1 Introduction

Numerous advancements in computer technology makes an automatic Facial Expression Recognition (FER) as an attractive research area for HMI. The knowledge about the facial parametric model is the prior requirement to recognize the expression status. The Facial Action Coding Systems (FACS) and the Facial Animation Parameters (FAP) [1] define the muscle actions and animations for standardized face parameterization. The utilization of 3D and 4D recordings [2] improves the ability of exploitation of facial information. The Local Diagonal Number (LDN) pattern [3] is the derived method from LDP that encodes the structural and intensity variations for specific face texture. The RGB-D images captured by low-cost sensors (Kinect) [4,5] extends the FER systems applicability into Human-Robot Interaction (HRI). Based on the properties of the image, the feature extraction is split up into two categories such as static image-based and the image sequence-based methods. Among them, the static methods utilize the fewer data to achieve the fast recognition whereas the sequence-based

© Springer Nature Singapore Pte Ltd. 2016
Z. Zhang and K. Huang (Eds.): IVS 2016, CCIS 664, pp. 107–113, 2016.
DOI: 10.1007/978-981-10-3476-3_13

methods requires more data. The Gabor Wavelet Transform (GWT) [11] that extracts the features in two domains namely, spatial and frequency from the static image that leads to high dimension. The existence of facial variations, pose, illumination and the cultural change causes the performance degradation in FER systems. Hence, there is a need of large-scale data to overcome the problems in FER. The introduction section addresses the major issues in the traditional FER methods such as the large scale data and the detailed information analysis. The technical contributions of proposed PBDP-GAM are listed as follows:

1. The Patch-Based Diagonal Pattern (PBDP) proposed in this paper supports the reliable detection and tracking of facial points that increases the size of labeled pool.
2. The incorporation of PBDP on Geometric Appearance Models (GAM) and the co-training extract the facial features in the multi-direction and the complementary information learning.
3. The multi-directional feature extraction and the maximization of labeled database by PBDP-GAM supports the detailed information analysis.

2   Related Work

The capture of facial surface deformations is the necessary stage in FER systems and it suffers from illumination variations. Ghosh and Ari [6] utilized the Gray World (GW) algorithm to overcome the illumination variation from grayscale and color images. An accurate prediction of scene illumination variation depends on the hand-crafted features that degraded the performance. Convolutional Neural Network (CNN) and Differential Mean Curvature Map (DMCM) multithreading cascade of rotation-invariant HOG (McRiHOG) and Dynamic Bayesian Network (DBN) captured the facial interactions in different levels such as bottom-top and top-bottom [7]. The two-way facial feature tracking algorithms have the great influence on expression/Action Unit recognition performance. Principal Component Analysis (PCA), Gray Level Co-occurrence Matrix (GLCM) and Fuzzy-logic based Image Dimensionality Reduction using the Shape Primitives (FIDRSP) reduced the gray level with efficient recognition. The existence of redundant and irrelevant features increased the complexity and the computational cost in classification algorithms. Feature selection methods, time-series classification methods, Relevance Vector Machine (RVM) [8], Output-Associative RVM (OA-RVM) and Continuous Conditional Neural Fields (CCNF) [10] predicted the multi-dimensional output vectors for the specific features and the spatial-temporal dependencies inclusion affected the robustness adversely. Hence, there is a need of large scale database to analyze the expressions. The evolution of Co-training methods [13] improved the recognition performance with the large size templates utilization.

3   Patch-Based Diagonal Pattern on Geometric Appearance Model

Figure 1 shows the working flow of PBDP-GAM. Initially, the preprocessing stage comprises noise removal and skin pixel detection from input RGB images in the KinectDB. The Gaussian filter removes the noise in the images. The Viola-Jones [9] method detects the face from the input RGB images.

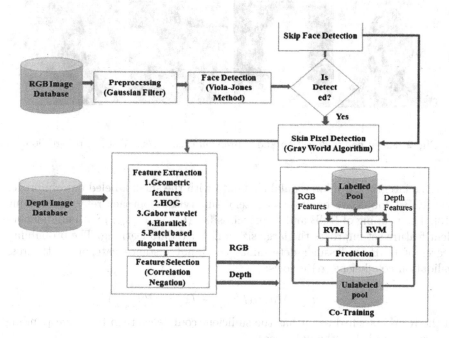

Fig. 1. Architecture of proposed method.

The GAM accepts the segmented skin pixels and converts them into binary to extract the top of the head pixel. Then, GAM predicts the nose, mouth, chin, and forehead from the top pixel by using distance measurement. The HOG, Gabor followed by GAM algorithm counts the gradient orientation occurrences for localized images and represents the image variations respectively. Then, we utilize the Haralick feature extraction for every 30-degree orientation that provides clear texture analysis. Based on diagonal pixel values, PBDP extracts image patterns. Initially, the image is divided into 3 * 3 matrix. The average of diagonal pixels is calculated. If the average pixel value is greater than the neighboring pixel, then the cell is filled with the value '1'. Otherwise, it is '0'. The count of ones and zeros decides the necessary patterns for RGB-D image. The likelihood estimation function in RVM classifier [8] identifies the facial expressions as neutral and smile for RGB-D images respectively. Figure 2(a)–(d) show the facial points detection. Figure 2(e)–(h) show the state of expression.

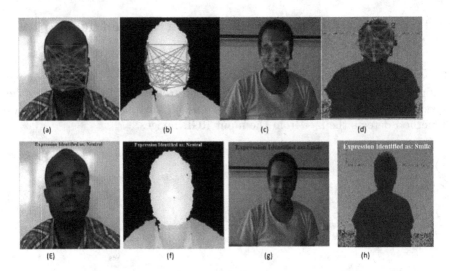

Fig. 2. Facial points detection and expression (neutral/smile state) recognition.

The integration of large unlabeled data with the small labeled data improves the RGB-D object recognition by a semi-supervised approach refers co-training [13]. The training of RGB and Depth classifier (C_{RGB}, C_{Depth}) with an independent feature set improves the large size unlabeled data learning. The probability scores of RGB-D classifier determines the input instance category with cross validation co-efficient (α) follows:

$$c = arg_{c_i \epsilon x} Max(\alpha P_{C_{RGB}}^{c_i} + (1 - \alpha) P_{C_{Depth}}^{c_i}) \tag{1}$$

If the RVM classified result has the sufficient confidence then the corresponding images are added to the database.

4   Performance Analysis

The EURECOMM and biographer database validates the effectiveness of proposed algorithm. The EURECOM dataset [13] contains facial images of 52 peoples (14 females, 38 males) captured by Kinect sensor in two sessions at different time periods. The Biographer-RGB-D database contains facial images of 13 peoples (Chinese males with an age of fewer than 30 years with 25 images of each) captured by the softKinetic camera with 15 fps frame rate.

4.1   Performance Metrics

The comparative analysis of proposed PBDP-GAM without co-training, with co-training and SVM classifier regarding True Positive (TP), True Negative (TN), False Positive (FP), False negative (FN), accuracy, sensitivity, specificity, precision, recall (True Positive Rate (TPR), Jaccard coefficient, Dice overlap, Kappa

Table 1. Parametric equations

Parameters	Descriptions
True Positive (TP)	Cases of correct predictions of expressions
True Negative (TN)	Cases of correct predictions of no expressions
False Positive (FP)	Cases of incorrect predictions of expressions
False Negative (FN)	Cases of incorrect predictions of no expression.
Accuracy	$(TP + TN)/(TP + TN + FP + FN)$
Sensitivity	$TP/(TP + FN)$
Specificity	$TN/(FP + TN)$
Precision	$TP/(TP + FP)$
Recall	$TP/(TP + FN)$
Dice coefficient	Measure of similarity between the expression sets
Jaccard coefficient	Size of intersection of expression sets/size of union of expression sets
Kappa coefficient	$k = \frac{P_0 - P_e}{1 - P_e}$

Table 2. Performance analysis

Performance metrics	PBDP-SVM	PBDP-RVM without co-training	PBDP-RVM with co-training
Sensitivity	86.2069	94.8276	98.2759
Specificity	99.2908	98.5816	99.2908
Precision	96.1538	93.2203	96.6102
Recall	86.2069	94.8276	98.2759
Jaccard coeff	97.0588	97.9412	99.1176
Dice overlap	98.5075	98.9599	99.5569
Kappa coeff	0.8916	0.9277	0.969
Accuracy	97.0588	97.94	99.12

coefficient on Biographer RGB-D database shows the effectiveness of proposed work. The performance parameters specify how the proposed algorithm recognizes the facial expression of the images. Table 1 describes the equations used to evaluate the performance parameters. Table 2 shows the estimated values for each performance metrics. The RVM combined with the PBDP approach effectively reduces the computational cost due to the generalized form.

Figure 3 shows the recognition and error rate analysis for various expression states over the existing methods. The PBDP-GAM offers 2.17, 14.92, 2.57, 6.65 and 3.89% improvement in recognition rate for smile, OM, SG, OH and OP respectively compared to SANN method [12]. Similarly, PBDP-GAM reduces the error rate by 36.87, 25.12, 74.78, 25.21, 50.97 and 45.87% compared to SANN respectively.

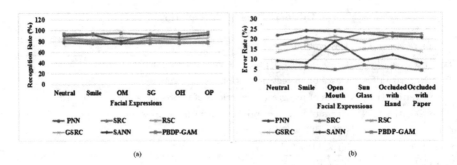

Fig. 3. (a) Recognition rate and (b) error rate analysis.

5   Conclusion

This paper addressed the limitation of real-time HMI-based applications such that the detailed information analysis that requires large scale labeled pool. The novel Patch-Based Diagonal Pattern (PBDP) on Geometric Appearance Models (GAM) are proposed that extracted the features on multiple direction for detailed information analysis. The co-training utilization created an effective large scale database with better identification and acceptance rate values. Finally, the application of Relevance Vector Machine (RVM) to the extracted features effectively classified the facial expression status. The experimental results of proposed PBDP-GAM show the efficient recognition performance over the existing methods regarding the recognition and the error rate values. Extension of this work includes the deep learning methods for 3D face FER system.

Acknowledgment. This work was supported by the National Natural Science Foundation of China under Grants 61473290, the National High Technology Research and Development Program of China (863 Program) under Grant 2015AA042307, and the international partnership program of Chinese Academy of Sciences, Grant No. 173211KYSB20160008.

References

1. Bettadapura, V.: Face expression recognition, analysis: the state of the art. arXiv preprint arXiv:1203.6722 (2012)
2. Sandbach, G., Zafeiriou, S., Pantic, M., Yin, L.: Static and dynamic 3D facial expression recognition: a comprehensive survey. Image Vis. Comput. **30**, 683–697 (2012)
3. Ramirez Rivera, A., Rojas, C., Oksam, C.: Local directional number pattern for face analysis: face and expression recognition. IEEE Trans. Image Process. **22**, 1740–1752 (2013)
4. Goswami, G., Bharadwaj, S., Vatsa, M., Singh, R.: On RGB-D face recognition using Kinect. In: IEEE Sixth International Conference on Biometrics: Theory, Applications and Systems (BTAS), pp. 1–6 (2013)

5. Romero, P., Cid, F., Núñez, P.: A novel real time facial expression recognition system based on Candide-3 reconstruction model. In: Proceedings of the XIV Workshop on Physical Agents (WAF 2013), Madrid, Spain, pp. 18–19 (2013)
6. Ghosh, D., Ari, S.: Static Hand Gesture Recognition Using Mixture of Features and SVM Classifier (2015)
7. Bianco, S., Cusano, C., Schettini, R.: Color constancy using CNNs. arXiv preprint arXiv:1504.04548 (2015)
8. Lemaire, P., Ardabilian, M., Liming, C., Daoudi, M.: Fully automatic 3D facial expression recognition using differential mean curvature maps and histograms of oriented gradients. In: 10th IEEE International Conference and Workshops on Automatic Face and Gesture Recognition (FG), pp. 1–7 (2013)
9. El Maghraby, A., Abdalla, M., Enany, O., El Nahas, M.Y.: Detect and analyze face parts information using Viola-Jones and geometric approaches. Int. J. Comput. Appl. **101**, 23–28 (2014)
10. Baltrušaitis, T., Robinson, P., Morency, L.-P.: Continuous conditional neural fields for structured regression. In: Fleet, D., Pajdla, T., Schiele, B., Tuytelaars, T. (eds.) ECCV 2014. LNCS, vol. 8692, pp. 593–608. Springer, Heidelberg (2014). doi:10.1007/978-3-319-10593-2_39
11. Ruan, J., Yin, J., Chen, Q., Chen, G.: Facial expression recognition based on gabor wavelet transform and relevance vector machine. J. Inf. Comput. Sci. **11**, 295–302 (2014)
12. Wong, Y., Harandi, M.T., Sanderson, C.: On robust face recognition via sparse coding: the good the bad and the ugly. IET Biom. **3**, 176–189 (2014)
13. Rui, M., Kose, N., Dugelay, J.L.: KinectFaceDB: a kinect database for face recognition. IEEE Trans. Syst. Man Cybern.: Syst. **44**, 1534–1548 (2014)

Multi-object Detection Based on Binocular Stereo Vision

Zhannan He[1], Qiang Ren[1], Tao Yang[1(✉)], Jing Li[2], and Yanning Zhang[1]

[1] School of Computer Science, Northwestern Polytechnical University, Xian, China
tyang@nwpu.edu.cn
[2] School of Telecommunications Engineering, Xidian University, Xian, China

Abstract. This paper proposes a new multi-object detection system based on binocular stereo vision. Firstly, we calibrate the two cameras to get intrinsic and extrinsic parameters and transformation matrix of the two cameras. Secondly, stereo rectify and stereo match is done to get a disparity map with image pairs acquired by binocular camera synchronously. Thus 3d coordinate of the objects is obtained. We then projects these 3D points to the ground to generate a top view projection image. Lastly, we propose distance and color based Mean shift cluster approach to classify the projected points, after which the number and position of objects can be determined. Binocular stereo vision based methods can overcome the problems of object occlusion, illumination variation, and shadow interference. Experiments in both indoor and corridor scenes show the advantages of the proposed system.

1 Introduction

Video surveillance is widely used in our life. It is very important in the area of public safety, traffic control, and intelligent human-machine interaction etc. How to detect multi objects accurately is one of the major concerned problems to the researchers. Monocular, binocular and multiple cameras are all used to detect objects. Existing object detection systems based on monocular vision [1–4] usually have problems in such conditions: (1) multiple objects with severe occlusion; (2) illumination variation; (3) the shadow interference. As for multi-camera based detection system [5,6], it can avoid occlusion because of multi-view and depth information. However, multi-camera based system needs additional processing, extra memory requirement, superfluous energy consumption, higher installation cost, and complex handling and implementation. For the above problems, binocular stereo vision based surveillance is a compromise between the above two systems. The binocular can solve occlusion problem and has a small computational cost and is easy to implement.

There is some work focus on stereo rectify [7,8] and stereo match [9]. Several approaches based on stereo vision have been proposed to solve object detection problems [10–16]. The work of Muñoz-Salinas et al. [10] combines information from multiple stereo cameras to get three different plan-view maps to detect objects. In [11], Cai et al. presents a new stereo vision-based model for

© Springer Nature Singapore Pte Ltd. 2016
Z. Zhang and K. Huang (Eds.): IVS 2016, CCIS 664, pp. 114–121, 2016.
DOI: 10.1007/978-981-10-3476-3_14

Fig. 1. The binocular stereo vision system. The left and right image are acquired by binocular stereo camera synchronously. The final result is Marked in right image with a stereo bounding box.

multi-object detection and tracking in surveillance system by projecting a sparse set of feature points to the ground plane. In [12], Schindler et al. study a system for detection and 3D localisation of people in street scene recorded from a mobile stereo rig. Colantonio et al. [13] uses a thermo-camera and two stereo visible-cameras synchronized to acquire multi-source information: three-dimensional data about target geometry, and its thermal information is combined to do object detection.

Our multi-object detection system based on binocular stereo vision is show in Fig. 1. It performs well when there exists severe occlusion, illumination variation and shadow interference. 3D coordinate of objects in the scene is obtained by binocular stereo vision, and then project it to the ground to get a top view projection image. In the projection image, the points on different objects are separated from each other so that object occlusion can be eliminated. In order to get the 3D coordinate of the object, the calibration of binocular stereo camera is needed. The framework of the proposed system is shown in Fig. 2.

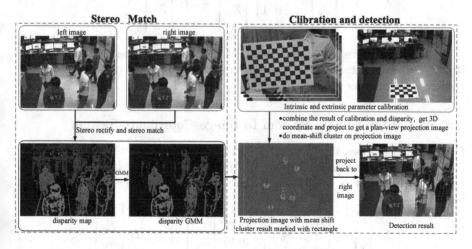

Fig. 2. The framework of the proposed binocular stereo vision system. Our work is divided into three main blocks: stereo match, calibration and detection.

The remainder of the paper is organised as follows: in Sect. 2 the calibration of binocular stereo camera is introduced. Section 3 describes the mean shift cluster method for object detection. Section 4 shows the result of out experiment. Conclusions and future works are contained in Sect. 5.

2   Binocular Stereo Vision System Calibration

In this part, we mainly talk about the camera calibration. Firstly, each camera is calibrated by Zhang's [17] planar calibration method and then rectified by Bouguet algorithm. Next, we match the same point in left and right images and get disparity map by BM algorithm. Through stereo calibration, we can get rotation and translation matrix which transforms the left camera coordinate system to the right camera coordinate system. Combining the disparity map between left and right images and calibration result, we can get the 3D coordinate of the object in the scene. The transformation of coordinate is introduced in detail below.

2.1   Camera Coordinate System to World Coordinate System

World coordinate is used to describe the position of camera, the rotation and translation matrixes between camera coordinate and world coordinate shown the transformation relationship between them. Assume that the point P's coordinate in the world coordinate system is (X_w, Y_w, Z_w), and its coordinate in the camera coordinate system is (X_c, Y_c, Z_c). According to geometric model of camera, select the right camera as the reference camera, as its center is the original point of the camera coordinate system. Hence:

$$
\begin{bmatrix} X_c \\ Y_c \\ Z_c \\ 1 \end{bmatrix} = \begin{bmatrix} R & T \\ \mathbf{0} & 1 \end{bmatrix} \begin{bmatrix} X_w \\ Y_w \\ Z_w \\ 1 \end{bmatrix} = M_1 \begin{bmatrix} X_w \\ Y_w \\ Z_w \\ 1 \end{bmatrix} \tag{1}
$$

Here we designate the original point of the world coordinate on the ground. R and T are the rotation and translation matrixes between camera coordinate system and world coordinate system.

2.2   World Coordinate System to Image Coordinate System

By the last step, we can get world coordinate of a point on the image. Assume that point P is the center of object on top view projection image, we need to reproject the point to the original right image to show the detection result, hence:

$$
Z_c \begin{bmatrix} u \\ v \\ 1 \end{bmatrix} = \begin{bmatrix} f_u & 0 & u_0 & 0 \\ 0 & f_v & v_0 & 0 \\ 0 & 0 & 1 & 0 \end{bmatrix} \begin{bmatrix} R & T \\ \mathbf{0} & 1 \end{bmatrix} \begin{bmatrix} X_w \\ Y_w \\ Z_w \\ 1 \end{bmatrix} = M_2 M_1 \begin{bmatrix} X_w \\ Y_w \\ Z_w \\ 1 \end{bmatrix} \tag{2}
$$

(u,v) is the coordinate of point P on right image. f_u and f_v are vertical and horizon focal length, M_2 is camera's intrinsic parameter matrix, M_1 is camera's extrinsic parameter matrix, which can be calibrated by Zhang's planar calibration method.

3 Object Detection - Mean Shift Cluster

After the binocular stereo camera calibration, we can get a projection image, in which each pixel represents one point on the ground and its value shows the quantity of points projected to the pixel. With the projection image, we can solve the object detection problem by clustering, as one cluster represents one object. We use a new distance and color based Mean shift cluster algorithm. Mean shift cluster [18,19] is a powerful non-parametric technique that does not require prior knowledge of the number of clusters and does not constrain the shape of the clusters.

The main idea behind Mean shift is to treat the points in the d-dimensional feature space as an empirical probability density function where dense regions in the feature space correspond to the local maxima or modes of the underlying distribution. It is a iterative algorithm. We use gradient ascent procedure on the local estimated density until convergence to solve the problem.

The mean shift procedure consists the following three steps:

1. choose an initial point as cluster center.
2. compute the mean shift vector from other points to this center.
3. move the center along the mean shift vector and get a new center, repeat step 1 until reach the termination condition.

When the two object are much close to each other, it is difficult to separate them by the distance based mean shift cluster.

Here we use both distance and color information of the projection image to do mean shift cluster. In this case, the kernel is $K_{h_s,h_c}(x)$ in Eq. 3.

$$K_{h_s,h_c}(x) = K\left(\left\|\frac{x^s - x_i^s}{h_s}\right\|\right)K\left(\left\|\frac{x^r - x_i^r}{h_r}\right\|\right) \tag{3}$$

To sum up, the steps are that the points are constantly moving along the direction of the probability density gradient. Mean Shift cluster can find the location of highest density by means of gradient descent.

We get n clusters centers by mean shift cluster method, each cluster represents one object. Then generate a bounding box, whose center is the cluster center. The object projection to the ground is inside the box. Combined with the height information of the object, we reproject these points back to the reference image. The detection result is shown in Fig. 3.

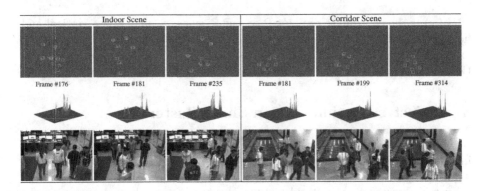

Fig. 3. The detection result by mean shift clustering. Top two rows are the 2D and 3D projection image, and the mean shift cluster results are marked with a white rectangle bounding box. Bottom row shows the detection result in original right image.

4 Experiment

In this section we show the performance of the proposed binocular stereo vision based multi-object detection system. We choose the point grey Bumblebee2 stereo vision camera (BB2-08S2C-60) and its baseline is 120 mm. The camera is placed in the ceiling with a certain angle. The area covered by the camera is 3 m × 4 m. The camera is synchronised and set to acquire images at 60 fps with a resolution of 1024 × 768 pixels. Our system has no specific requirements for the surveillance objects, and moving people is used as an example of multi-object detection in both indoor and corridor scenes, eight person are asked to walk casually.

Figure 4 shows a comparison between our system and four typical background model based methods, including AdaptiveBL [20], DP MeanBGS, Multi-LayerBG (MLBG) [21], Mixture of Gaussian V1BGS (MGV1BG) [20]. The detection results are marked with red stereo bounding boxes. It shows that our method can detect the occluded objects while other methods can't. Different objects are separate when the occlusion happens on the projection image.

Fig. 4. Comparison to four background model based object detection methods. (Color figure online)

However, background model based methods can't separate them, as occluded objects and other objects are fused together and form a connected domain on the image.

4.1 Indoor Scene Experiment

The indoor scene always placed many things, like desks, cupboards etc., and presents a complex background on the image. Our system is a good solution to occlusion problem and complex background, as the object detection is solved by distance and color combined mean shift cluster on the top view projection image. The left part of Fig. 3 shows the detection result in indoor scenes. We can see that even though some objects are severely occluded, however, they can be detected properly. The detection results are marked with a red stereo bounding box.

4.2 Corridor Scene Experiment

As everyone knows, the corridor don't have sufficient light and the image quality is not good, especially at night. When people walking in the scene, severe occlusion, illumination and shadow change may happen. The state of art method based on monocular does not work well on this data set, but our method shows great performance.

We tested with 166 frames of indoor scene, 704 total number of real objects and 166 frames of corridor scene, 872 total number of real objects. In indoor scene experiment, only 21 real objects are not detected and there are 4 false alarms. In corridor scene experiment, our method also performs well, 25 real objects are not detected and there are 27 false alarms. The evaluation illustrates that our method shows high detection rate and low false detection rate.

5   Conclusions

In this paper, we present a multi-object detection system based on binocular stereo vision. 3D coordinate of object can be obtained by the binocular stereo vision based method. Then we can get a top view projection image. Mean shift cluster is used to determine the number and position of each object in the scene. Experiment in both indoor and corridor scenes shows that our method performs well to solve the problem of occlusion, illumination change and shadow interference. In future, we will make efforts to do track on this system.

Acknowledgements. This work is supported by the National Natural Science Foundation of China (No. 61672429, No. 61502364, No. 61272288, No. 61231016), ShenZhen Science and Technology Foundation (JCYJ20160229172932237), Northwestern Polytechnical University (NPU) New AoXiang Star (No. G2015KY0301), Fundamental Research Funds for the Central Universities (No. 3102015AX007), NPU New People and Direction (No. 13GH014604).

References

1. Szegedy, C., Toshev, A., Erhan, D.: Deep neural networks for object detection. In: Advances in Neural Information Processing Systems, pp. 2553–2561 (2013)
2. Tang, S., Andriluka, M., Schiele, B.: Detection and tracking of occluded people. Int. J. Comput. Vis. **110**(1), 58–69 (2014)
3. Girshick, R., Donahue, J., Darrell, T., Malik, J.: Rich feature hierarchies for accurate object detection and semantic segmentation. In: Proceedings of the IEEE Conference on Computer Vision and Pattern Recognition, pp. 580–587 (2014)
4. Ren, S., He, K., Girshick, R., Sun, J.: Faster R-CNN: towards real-time object detection with region proposal networks. In: Advances in Neural Information Processing Systems, pp. 91–99 (2015)
5. Zhang, S., Wang, C., Chan, S.-C., Wei, X., Ho, C.-H.: New object detection, tracking, and recognition approaches for video surveillance over camera network. Sens. J. IEEE **15**(5), 2679–2691 (2015)
6. Raman, R., Sa, P.K., Majhi, B.: Occlusion prediction algorithms for multi-camera network. In: 2012 Sixth International Conference on Distributed Smart Cameras (ICDSC), pp. 1–6. IEEE (2012)
7. Kowalczuk, J., Psota, E.T., Perez, L.C.: Real-time stereo matching on CUDA using an iterative refinement method for adaptive support-weight correspondences. IEEE Trans. Circuits Syst. Video Technol. **23**(1), 94–104 (2013)
8. Nguyen, D.M., Hanca, J., Lu, S.-P., Munteanu, A.: Robust stereo matching using census cost, discontinuity-preserving disparity computation and view-consistent refinement. In: 2015 International Conference on 3D Imaging (IC3D), pp. 1–8. IEEE (2015)
9. Park, J., Choi, J., Seo, B.-K., Park, J.-I.: Fast stereo image rectification using mobile GPU. In: The Third International Conference on Digital Information Processing and Communications, pp. 485–488. The Society of Digital Information and Wireless Communication (2013)
10. Muñoz-Salinas, R., Medina-Carnicer, R., Madrid-Cuevas, F.J., Carmona-Poyato, A.: People detection and tracking with multiple stereo cameras using particle filters. J. Vis. Commun. Image Represent. **20**(5), 339–350 (2009)
11. Cai, L., He, L., Yiren, X., Zhao, Y., Yang, X.: Multi-object detection and tracking by stereo vision. Pattern Recogn. **43**(12), 4028–4041 (2010)
12. Schindler, K., Ess, A., Leibe, B., Van Gool, L.: Automatic detection and tracking of pedestrians from a moving stereo rig. ISPRS J. Photogramm. Remote Sens. **65**(6), 523–537 (2010)
13. Colantonio, S., Benvenuti, M., Di Bono, M.G., Pieri, G., Salvetti, O.: Object tracking in a stereo and infrared vision system. Infrared Phys. Technol. **49**(3), 266–271 (2007)
14. Kelly, P.: Pedestrian detection and tracking using stereo vision techniques. Ph.D. thesis, Dublin City University (2007)
15. Jafari, O.H., Mitzel, D., Leibe, B.: Real-time RGB-D based people detection and tracking for mobile robots and head-worn cameras. In: 2014 IEEE International Conference on Robotics and Automation (ICRA), pp. 5636–5643. IEEE (2014)
16. Hegger, F., Hochgeschwender, N., Kraetzschmar, G.K., Ploeger, P.G.: People detection in 3d Point clouds using local surface normals. In: Chen, X., Stone, P., Sucar, L.E., Zant, T. (eds.) RoboCup 2012. LNCS (LNAI), vol. 7500, pp. 154–165. Springer, Heidelberg (2013). doi:10.1007/978-3-642-39250-4_15

17. Zhang, Z.: A flexible new technique for camera calibration. IEEE Trans. Pattern Anal. Mach. Intell. **22**(11), 1330–1334 (2000)
18. Tao, W., Jin, H., Zhang, Y.: Color image segmentation based on mean shift and normalized cuts. IEEE Trans. Syst. Man Cybern. Part B: Cybern. **37**(5), 1382–1389 (2007)
19. Cheng, Y.: Mean shift, mode seeking, and clustering. IEEE Trans. Pattern Anal. Mach. Intell. **17**(8), 790–799 (1995)
20. KaewTraKulPong, P., Bowden, R.: An improved adaptive background mixture model for real-time tracking with shadow detection. In: Remagnino, P., Jones, G.A., Paragios, N., Regazzoni, C.S. (eds.) Video-Based Surveillance Systems, pp. 135–144. Springer, Heidelberg (2002)
21. Yao, J., Odobez, J.-M.: Multi-layer background subtraction based on color and texture. In: IEEE Conference on Computer Vision and Pattern Recognition, CVPR 2007, pp. 1–8. IEEE (2007)

Fast Vehicle Detection in Satellite Images Using Fully Convolutional Network

Jingao Hu[✉], Tingbing Xu, Jixiang Zhang, and Yiping Yang

Institute of Automation, Chinese Academy of Sciences, Beijing 100190, China
{hujingao2014,xutingbing2014,jixiang.zhang,yiping.yang}@ia.ac.cn

Abstract. Detecting small targets like vehicles in high resolution satellite images is a significant but challenging task. In the past decade, some detection frameworks have been proposed to solve this problem. However, like the traditional ways of object detection in natural images those methods all consist of multiple separated stages. Region proposals are first produced, then, fed into the feature extractor and classified finally. Multi-stage detection schemes are designed complicated and time-consuming. In this paper, we propose a unified single-stage vehicle detection framework using fully convolutional network (FCN) to simultaneously predict vehicle bounding boxes and class probabilities from an arbitrary-sized satellite image. We elaborate our FCN architecture which replaces the fully connected layers in traditional CNNs with convolutional layers and design vehicle object-oriented training methodology with reference boxes (anchors). The whole model can be trained end-to-end by minimizing a multi-task loss function. Comparison experiment results on a common dataset demonstrate that our FCN model which has much fewer parameters can achieve a faster detection with lower false alarm rates compared to the traditional methods.

1 Introduction

Recent advances in remote sensing imagery make high-resolution satellite images more accessible. Detecting vehicle objects in those satellite images becomes an essential and meaningful research field for it can provide important information for homeland surveillance, intelligent transportation planning, disaster search and rescue, etc. Although a lot of works have been done, there is no one that takes efficiency, robustness and speed all in consideration.

Machine learning methods are widely utilised in the research of satellite image vehicle detection in the past decade. Like traditional object detection frameworks in natural images those methods mainly take three stages. Region proposals (latent candidates) are first produced by certain proposal extracting algorithm like selective search and BING, then, fed into the feature extractor and classified finally. Zhao and Nevatia [1] take vehicle detection as a 3D object recognition problem so they select the boundary of the car body, front windshield and the shadow as features which are then integrated by a Bayesian network. Eikvil et al. [2] utilise satellite image information like road information, geometric-shape properties to assist their Hu moment-based detection method. Liang

© Springer Nature Singapore Pte Ltd. 2016
Z. Zhang and K. Huang (Eds.): IVS 2016, CCIS 664, pp. 122–129, 2016.
DOI: 10.1007/978-981-10-3476-3_15

et al. [3] propose a detection scheme that uses multiple kernel SVM (MKL-SVM) with HOG and Haar features. They trained MKL-SVM to learn an optimal kernel with many base kernels in order to get the trade-off between HOG and Haar features. Kembhavi et al. [4] construct an vehicle detection framework by extracting HOG, color probability maps and pairs of pixel as features and using a partial least square model.

All the detection framework we talk above are based on manual designed features. Such hand-crafted features are "shallow" for they mainly consider color, edge and general shape of the object and since real scene can be very complex and various, those features reach a bottleneck in recognition discrimination and robustness. Since Krizhevsky et al. [5] made a breakthrough using a convolutional neural network (CNN) in ILSVRC [6] in 2012, CNN as an deep learning model has been widely used in visual recognition tasks and yielded superior performance. Deep convolutional neural networks can automatically learn rich hierarchical features from raw data with its convolution layers and pooling layers and then send those self-learned features to an multiple layer perceptron (MLP) for classification or regression. Jiang et al. [7] use graph-based superpixel segmentation to extract region proposals and train a CNN to classify those proposals. Chen et al. [8] slide a window to get vehicle proposals and train a hybrid deep neural network (HDNN) to do the recognition work. Chen et al. [9] also design another type of deep neural network called parallel deep convolutional neural network to do the vehicle detection work.

Until now, all the detection framework we have discussed consist of at least two stages which means complicatedly designed and time-consuming for proposal generation process is hardly realized on GPU. For further acceleration, several newly proposed proposal methods based on convolutional features, such as region proposal network (RPN) [10], MultiBox [11] and DeepMask [12] are very suitable for implementation on GPU. Inspired by region proposal network [10], we propose a unified single-stage vehicle detection framework using fully convolutional network which can be trained end-to-end. We elaborate our FCN architecture which can process arbitrary-sized images and design the training methodology in experiment. The comparison results demonstrate that our method can achieve a faster detection with lower false alarm rates and much fewer parameters compared to traditional methods. The remainder of this paper is presented as follows. Firstly, we explain our method in Sect. 2, in Sect. 3, we present and analyse our experiment results. We conclude our work in Sect. 4.

2   Method

In this section, we explain our model architecture and learning methodology respectively. We use a fully convolutional network (FCN) [13] which takes a satellite image of any size as input and generates feature maps. Then the feature maps are sent to two sibling convolutional layers: a classification layer (cls.) and a box-regression layer (reg.). To reduce the number of candidate windows, like RPN [10] We use n reference boxes (also called anchors [10]) to hypothesize the vehicle objects' positions. The classification layer outputs the probability how likely one anchor covers an object and the box-regression layer outputs the regressed positions.

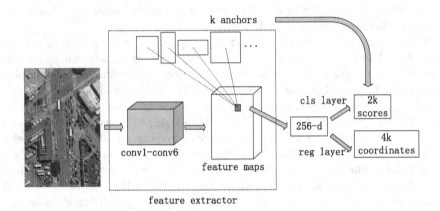

Fig. 1. Our FCN-based detection framework. The input is a arbitrary-sized raw satellite image of 3 channels. A CNN of 6 convolution layers acts as a feature extractor. The two sibling parts, classification layer and regression layer do the following detection work. We use k anchors to hypothesize the vehicle locations

2.1   Architecture of FCN

The architecture of FCN used in this paper is showed in Fig. 1. It consists of an feature extraction part and two sibling parts: classification and regression. In our experiments we investigate Zeiler and Fergus's model [14] which has 5 convolutional layers and 2 fully connected layers. ZF-net is designed for the ILSVRC classification competition [6] which has 1000 categories. As for detection task, it is not suitable for fully connected layers lose spatial information. So we replace the fully connected layers with convolutional layers, forming a single fully convolutional network. For clarity we demonstrate our FCN in Table 1. The FCN model has six 3×3 convolutional layers and 2 sibling 1×1 convolutional layers. Every spatial position (corresponding to a region of the input image) of conv6 feature map obtains a 256-d feature vector, which is fed into the box-classification layer (cls.) and box-regression layer. Our model has the same depth with ZF-net but much fewer parameters. In practice, we compared our fully convolutional network model with ZF-net model and found that our model is 14 times smaller.

2.2   Learning Methodology

To narrow the vehicle object searching space, we use several reference windows (anchors [10]) instead of searching every scale and aspect ratio. At training

Table 1. FCN configurations. For each convolutional layer "parameters" gives the filter size and the stride which the filter is sliding with and "filter numbers" gives the convolution kernel numbers of that layer. The pooling layers, LRN layers and ReLU activation layers are not shown for brevity

Layer	conv1	conv2	conv3	conv4	conv5	conv6	cls	reg
Parameters	$3 \times 3, 2$	$3 \times 3, 2$	$3 \times 3, 1$	$3 \times 3, 1$	$3 \times 3, 1$	$3 \times 3, 1$	$1 \times 1, 1$	$1 \times 1, 1$
Filter numbers	96	256	384	384	256	256	18	36

stage, our FCN model takes an arbitrary-sized image of 3 channels as input and generates feature maps of 256 channels after layer conv6. So in each position (x, y) of those features maps we can extract a 256-dimension vector corresponding to k anchors in the original image. If one anchor has intersection-over-union (IoU) overlap with any ground-truth box higher than 0.75 we take it as a positive sample and similarly, if the IoU is lower than 0.3 we consider it as a negative sample. Other reference boxes do not server as training examples. For anchors we use three 3 scales with box areas of 36×36, 44×44, and 50×50 pixels, and 3 aspect ratios of 2:1, 1:1, and 1:2. The 9 anchors we use are shown in Table 2.

Table 2. anchors

36^2, 2:1	36^2, 1:1	36^2, 1:2	44^2, 2:1	44^2, 1:1	44^2, 1:2	50^2, 2:1	50^2, 1:1	50^2, 1:2
50×26	36×36	26×50	62×31	44×44	31×62	70×36	50×50	36×70

Our FCN model is trained end-to-end by back-propagation (BP) [15] and the optimization scheme we use is stochastic gradient descent (SGD) [15]. We define our multi-task loss function following [16]:

$$L(\{p_i\}, \{t_i\}) = \frac{1}{N_{cls}} \sum_i L_{cls}(p_i, p_i^*) + \lambda \frac{1}{N_{reg}} \sum_i p_i^* L_{reg}(t_i, t_i^*). \tag{1}$$

Here, i is the index of anchors in a mini-batch and p_i is the predicted probability of anchor i being an object. The corresponding ground-truth label of p_i is p_i^* which is 1 if the anchor is positive and 0 otherwise. Similarly, t_i is the 4 predicted parameterized coordinates of the predicted bounding box and t_i^* the ground-truth. The classification loss L_{cls} is a vehicle vs. non-vehicle log loss and we use smooth function defined in [16] for regression loss L_{reg}. The hyperparameter λ controls the balance between the two task losses. We find that satisfactory results can be obtained for vehicle detection by setting $\lambda = 10$. Thus we keep this parameter fixed in the following experiments. Our implementation is based on Caffe [17] and Python.

3 Experiment

This part dispatches details of our experiment results. Specifically, we first introduce our dataset and then we compare the detection accuracy of our method with that of some typical methods. Finally our method is compared to other DNN-based methods on the subject of size and speed.

The dataset we use is that of [8] which includes 63 satellite images (1368 × 972) from google earth of San Francisco city containing 6887 vehicle samples. To guarantee adequate training data, we split the dataset to 46 and 17 for training and testing randomly. At training stage, we augment the training set by rotating the images by 90°, 180°, 270° and flipping the images horizontally. No further data augmentation is done. When training, parameters of conv1-conv5 are initialized from a pre-trained model on PASCAL VOC2007 detection task. We iterate 10000 times with learning rate 0.001 for the first 7000 mini-batches and 0.0001 for the next 3000 mini-batches on our training set. The momentum and weight decay we use are 0.9 and 0.0005 respectively [5].

Here the false alarm rate (FAR), precision rate (PR), and recall rate (RR) are defined as

$$\begin{cases} FAR = \dfrac{number\ of\ false\ alarms}{number\ of\ vehicles} \times 100\% \\ PR = \dfrac{number\ of\ detected\ vehicles}{number\ of\ detected\ objects} \times 100\% \ . \\ RR = \dfrac{number\ of\ detected\ vehicles}{number\ of\ vehicles} \times 100\% \end{cases} \qquad (2)$$

Table 3. FAR and processing time of our method and other methods on vehicle test set

Method	FAR at given RR (%)					
	95%	90%	85%	80%	75%	70%
Proposed	**19.3**	**9.38**	**5.42**	**3.53**	**2.27**	**1.63**
HDNN [8]	20.2	9.57	5.49	3.57	2.31	1.65
HOG+SVM [18]	67.5	43.4	29.3	20.2	14.3	10.3
LBP+SVM [19]	87.6	59.2	43.0	32.8	24.5	19.4
Adaboost [20]	91.6	65.3	49.1	40.1	31.6	25.8
Test time for one image (s)						
Proposed GPU	**0.2**					
HDNN [8] GPU	8					

In Table 3, we list the FAR at given RR of our method and 4 other typical methods. Our method outperforms other methods. It means our detector is more robust for it can detect objects which are very hard for the rest methods and that proves the benefits of deep convolutional features and position regression. In Fig. 2, we give some detection results samples. The testing images cover scenes from road with many trees to parking lot. Our detector performs very well even vehicle objects are quite dense on parking pot or sheltered by trees.

Fig. 2. Some detection results in San Francisco. The four images cover scenes from road with trees to parking lot

Since our detection framework is designed to be a single-stage detector, it also has a very fast speed. In Table 3, we give the processing time of one image of FCN and traditional DNN method. Our detector achieves a frame rate of 5 fps on a computer with NVIDIA GTX960. There are two main reasons that our method is superior in speed. One is discarding proposal extraction stage which is an essential step of the rest methods and the other is that we do convolutions to the whole original image to extract features rather than one proposal by another. So for one testing image, our network does forward propagation only once while the other methods need to do it hundreds or thousands times depending on how many region proposals they extract in the region proposals extracting stage.

Table 4. Size of parameters in various models

Model	AlexNet [5]	ZF-Net [14]	**Proposed**
Size	224 MB	249 MB	**17 MB**

Table 4 shows the comparison of parameter size for various models. Our FCN model is based on ZF-Net but the size is only 1/14 of ZF-Net which demonstrates that using convolutional layers instead of fully connected layers can greatly reduce the the amount of model parameters while obtaining comparable detection performance.

4   Conclusion

In this paper, we propose a new automatic satellite vehicle detection framework based on fully convolutional network (FCN). Different from traditional manual feature-based or DNN-based methods which are designed multi-stages, our method takes only one stage both in training and testing. By elaborating the FCN architecture and integrating several learning tricks, a very robust and fast vehicle detector is obtained. Our experiment results show that our approach achieves better performance in both detection accuracy and speed in comparison to alternative approaches with much fewer parameters.

References

1. Zhao, T., Nevatia, R.: Car detection in low resolution aerial images. Image Vis. Comput. **2**, 693–703 (2003)
2. Eikvil, L., Aurdal, L., Koren, H.: Classification-based vehicle detection in high-resolution satellite images. ISPRS J. Photogram. Remote Sens. **64**, 65–72 (2009)
3. Liang, P., Teodoro, G., Ling, H., Blasch, E., Chen, G., Bai, L.: Multiple kernel learning for vehicle detection in wide area motion imagery. In: Proceedings of the 15th International Conference on Information Fusion, pp. 1629–1636 (2012)
4. Kembhavi, A., Harwood, D., Davis, L.S.: Vehicle detection using partial least squares. IEEE Trans. Pattern Anal. Mach. Intell. **33**, 1250–1265 (2011)
5. Krizhevsky, A., Sutskever, I., Hinton, G.: Imagenet classification with deep convolutional neural networks. Adv. Neural Inf. Process. Syst. **25** (2012)
6. Russakovsky, O., Deng, J., Su, H., Krause, J., Satheesh, S., Ma, S., Huang, Z., Karpathy, A., Khosla, A., Bernstein, M., Berg, A.C., Fei-Fei, L.: Imagenet large scale visual recognition challenge. Int. J. Comput. Vis. **115**, 211–252 (2015)
7. Jiang, Q., Cao, L., Cheng, M., Wang, C., Li, J.: Deep neural networks-based vehicle detection in satellite images. In: International Symposium on Bioelectronics and Bioinformatics, pp. 184–187 (2015)
8. Chen, X., Xiang, S., Liu, C., Pan, C.: Vehicle detection in satellite images by hybrid deep convolutional neural networks. IEEE Geosci. Remote Sens. Lett. **11**, 1797–1801 (2014)
9. Chen, X., Xiang, S., Liu, C., Pan, C.: Vehicle detection in satellite images by parallel deep convolutional neural networks. In: Proceedings of the 2nd IAPR Asian Conference on Pattern Recognition, vol. 14, pp. 181–185 (2013)
10. Ren, S., He, K., Girshick, R., Sun, J.: Faster R-CNN: towards real-time object detection with region proposal networks. Adv. Neural Inf. Process. Syst. 91–99 (2015)
11. Szegedy, C., Reed, S., Erhan, D., Anguelov, D.: Scalable, high-quality object detection. arXiv:1412.1441 (v1) (2015)
12. Pinheiro, P., Collobert, R., Dollar, P.: Learning to segment object candidates. In: NIPS (2015)
13. Long, J., Shelhamer, E., Darrell, T.: Fully convolutional networks for semantic segmentation. In: Proceedings of the IEEE Conference on Computer Vision and Pattern Recognition, pp. 3431–3440 (2015)
14. Zeiler, M.D., Fergus, R.: Visualizing and understanding convolutional networks. In: Fleet, D., Pajdla, T., Schiele, B., Tuytelaars, T. (eds.) ECCV 2014. LNCS, vol. 8689, pp. 818–833. Springer, Heidelberg (2014). doi:10.1007/978-3-319-10590-1_53

15. LeCun, Y., Boser, B., Denker, J.S., Henderson, D., Howard, R.E., Hubbard, W., Jackel, L.D.: Backpropagation applied to handwritten zip code recognition. Neural Comput. 1, 541–551 (1989)
16. Girshick, R.: Fast R-CNN. In: Proceedings of the IEEE International Conference on Computer Vision, pp. 1440–1448 (2015)
17. Jia, Y., Shelhamer, E., Donahue, J., Karayev, S., Long, J., Girshick, R., Guadarrama, S., Darrell, T.: Caffe: convolutional architecture for fast feature embedding. In: Proceedings of the 22nd ACM International Conference on Multimedia, pp. 675–678 (2014)
18. Dalal, D., Triggs, B.: Histogram of oriented gradients for human detection. Proc. IEEE Conf. Comput. Vis. Pattern Recogn. 1, 886–893 (2005)
19. Ojala, T., Pietikainen, M., Maenpaa, T.: Multiresolution gray scale and rotation invariant texture classification with local binary patterns. IEEE Trans. Pattern Anal. Mach. Intell. 24, 971–987 (2002)
20. Viola, P., Jones, M.J.: Robust real-time face detection. Int. J. Comput. Vis. 57, 137–154 (2004)

Behavior, Activities, Crowd Analysis

Semi-supervised Hessian Eigenmap
for Human Action Recognition

Xueqi Ma, Jiaxing Pan, Yue Wang, and Weifeng Liu[(✉)]

China University of Petroleum (East China), Qingdao, China
liuwf@upc.edu.cn

Abstract. Dimensionality reduction has been attracting emerging attention with the explosive growing of high-dimensional data in many areas including web image annotation, video object detection, and human action recognition. Comparing with the traditional nonlinear dimensional reduction such as Locally Linear Embedding, Isometric feature Mapping, Laplacian Eigenmap, semi-supervised nonlinear dimensional reduction method can improve stability of the solution by taking into account prior information. In this paper, we integrate exact mapping information of certain data points into Hessian Eigenmap and propose semi-supervised Hessian Eigenmap. Considering the prior information with physical meaning, semi-supervised Hessian Eigenmap can approximate global low dimensional coordinates. On the other hand, Hessian can exploit high-order information of the local geometry of data distribution in comparison with graph Laplacian and thus further boost the performance. We conduct experiments on both synthetic and real world datasets. The experimental results demonstrate that the proposed semi-supervised Hessian Eigenmap algorithm outperforms the representative semi-supervised Laplacian Eigenmap algorithm.

1 Introduction

With the development of visual surveillance, many computer vision applications are attracting emerging attentions including web image annotation, video object detection, *etc.* In most cases, the visual information is represented by high-dimensional data. Therefore, it has been becoming important for dimensional reduction which aims to learn a suitable low-dimensional representation of the high-dimensional data.

The representative dimensional reduction methods include principal component analysis (PCA), multidimensional scaling (MDS), locally linear embedding (LLE), ISOMAP, local tangent space alignment (LTSA), Laplacian Eigenmap (LE) and Hessian Eigenmap (HE). Principal component analysis (PCA) [1] can transform the original data into a lower dimensional space and keep the most variance. Multidimensional scaling (MDS) [2] pictures the structure of a set of data points using Euclidean space and remains the distance of those points in low-dimensional space. Locally linear embedding (LLE) [3] aims to recover the global nonlinear structure from a set of locally linear patches. ISOMAP [4] builds on classical MDS but seeks to preserve the intrinsic geometry of the data, and it tries to use geodesic manifold distance to replace typical Euclidean distance between all pairs of data points. Local tangent space alignment (LTSA) [5] tries to find the global low-dimensional

© Springer Nature Singapore Pte Ltd. 2016
Z. Zhang and K. Huang (Eds.): IVS 2016, CCIS 664, pp. 133–139, 2016.
DOI: 10.1007/978-981-10-3476-3_16

coordinates by the local tangent space information. Laplacian Eigenmap [6] wants to find a low-dimensional representation for original high-dimensional data by maintaining the local properties which calculated by pairwise distance between neighboring points. And Hessian Eigenmap [7] is the method which achieves local linear embedding by minimizing the Hessian function on the manifold and the local Hessian is estimated by the local tangent space.

All the above traditional dimensional reduction methods are unsupervised, in which no prior information of the input data are taken into account. Recently, semi-supervised nonlinear dimensionality reduction [8] considered prior information for dimensional reduction and yielded global low dimensional coordinates with physical meaning. And then semi-supervised Laplacian Eigenmap (SSLE) [9] boosted the performance by integrating prior information into Laplacian Eigenmap. In this paper, we propose semi-supervised Hessian Eigenmap (SSHE) for human action recognition. In contrast to Laplacian, Hessian has a richer null-space and can exploit high-order information of the local geometry of data distribution. And Hessian extrapolates nicely to unseen data [10]. Firstly, we conduct experiments on synthesis data and a toy dataset (MNIST) to verify the proposed algorithm. Then we apply the proposed semi-supervised Hessian Eigenmap for human action recognition. The experimental results demonstrate that the proposed semi-supervised Hessian Eigenmap outperforms the semi-supervised Laplacian Eigenmap algorithm.

The rest of the paper is organized as follows. In Sect. 2, we briefly introduce the Hessian Eigenmap and then describe the semi-supervised Hessian Eigenmap in detail. In Sect. 3, we demonstrate the experiments on different datasets. And finally, the conclusion is drawn in Sect. 4.

2 Semi-supervised Hessian Eigenmap

In this section, we briefly introduce the procedure of Hessian Eigenmap at first. And then we describe the proposed semi-supervised Hessian Eigenmap.

2.1 Hessian Eigenmap

Suppose we are given a dataset $X = \{x_1, x_2, \ldots, x_n\}$ with n samples. Hessian Eigenmap algorithm can be summarized as the following four steps.

Step 1: Neighborhood construction. Using k-neighborhood to define neighbors in Euclidean distance for each input point x_i, we get neighborhood matrix N_i.

Step 2: Create local tangent coordinates. Conduct singular value decomposition on neighborhood matrix $N_i = U'DV$. The first d columns of V ($V_i = [v_1, v_2, \ldots, v_d]$) mean the tangent coordinates of data points x_i.

Step 3: Build local Hessian Estimator. First construct a column vector $1 = \left[\underbrace{1, 1, \ldots, 1}_{k}\right]'$ and a matrix $Q_i = [v_i \boxtimes v_j]_{1 \le i \le j \le d}$. Apply Gram-Schmidt procedure on the mixed matrix $[1, V_i, Q_i]$ and gain its orthogonalization matrix, then we extract a subset W_i at the same position of Q_i from it. Let $W_i = W_i \times W_i'$.

Step 4: Construct Hessian Eigenmap matrix. Let H is a $n \times n$ zero matrix, and fills matrix H through function $H(N_i, N_i) = H(N_i, N_i) + W_i$. Up to now, we calculate the first $d+1$ smallest eigenvalues of matrix H which are the low-dimensional embedding coordinates of the original high-dimensional data.

2.2 Semi-supervised Hessian Eigenmap

In this part, we discuss about Semi-Supervised Hessian Eigenmap. Let dataset $X = \{x_1, x_2, \ldots, x_n\} = [X_1 X_2]$, subset $X_1 = \{x_1, x_2, \ldots, x_m\}$ and $X_2 = \{x_{m+1}, \ldots, x_n\}$ $s.t. m < n$. Suppose that X_1 is a part of dataset X whose low dimensional coordinates are already known while X_2 is the rest. Also we divide the low dimensional coordinate matrix Y into $Y = [Y_1 Y_2]$, in which Y_1 corresponds to X_1, while Y_2 in accordance with X_2.

Similar to the unsupervised Hessian Eigenmap, we use the Donoho & Grimes's method [7] to get the Hessian matrix H. Then similar to SSLE [9], we divide H into

$$H = \begin{bmatrix} H_{11} & H_{12} \\ H_{21} & H_{22} \end{bmatrix} \tag{1}$$

Where H_{11} is of size $m \times m$. Since Y_1 is known, we can get Y_2 by solving the minimization problem:

$$min_{Y_2} [Y_1 \quad Y_2] \begin{bmatrix} H_{11} & H_{12} \\ H_{21} & H_{22} \end{bmatrix} \begin{bmatrix} Y_1^T \\ Y_2^T \end{bmatrix} \tag{2}$$

Compared with SSLE, we just use the Hessian to replace the Laplacian. Then the minimization function equals to

$$min_{Y_2} \left(Y_1 H_{11} Y_1^T + Y_2 H_{12}^T Y_1^T + Y_1 H_{12} Y_2^T + Y_2 H_{22} Y_2^T \right) \tag{3}$$

So the answer given by the partial derivative of the function above sub Y_2 and let it equals to zero.

$$\frac{\partial \left(Y_1 H_{11} Y_1^T + Y_2 H_{12}^T Y_1^T + Y_1 H_{12} Y_2^T + Y_2 H_{22} Y_2^T \right)}{\partial Y_2} = 0 \overset{obtain}{\Rightarrow} H_{22} Y_2^T + H_{11}^T Y_1^T = 0 \tag{4}$$

Now, Y_2 can be figured out easily for Y_1 is supported by supervised points X_1.

3   Experiments

In this section we conduct experiments on both synthetic and real world datasets. The representative SSLE and the proposed SSHE are compared in Sects 3.1 and 3.3, also traditional unsupervised algorithms LE and HE are involved in our comparison for visual effects in Sect 3.2. And in the semi-supervised methods, the label information of prior points defined by one hot code. Most importantly, the neighboring number k is chosen carefully for reaching the best performance of each algorithm while the other parameters staying the same. In Sects. 3.1 and 3.3, a simple classifier [9] is designed as $Label_i = arg_{j=1,2,...,N} max Y_2^i(j), i = 1, 2, ..., (n - m)$, N is the class number of input data, and Y_2^i means the calculated low dimensional coordinate matrix for the rest data. What we need to do is to find which line gets the largest number, then that line number corresponds to the label information. By comparing the returned labels with the real labels, we can get the accuracy rate.

3.1   Experiments on Swiss Roll

Dataset and Experiment Setting: Swiss Roll is a common synthetic data model in manifold learning. In this experiment, we create a 3000 points Swiss Roll with 2 categories (each category owns about 1500 points). We reduce the dimensionality to 2D, while the original dimensionality reaching to 3D. The supervised points are selected randomly and each class has the same number of prior points. The label information of supervised points are defined as [1 0] for the first class and [0 1] for the other one. We retry 10 times on each set of parameters, then average them as the final results. Both SSLE and SSHE are applied to this dataset. The result of the experiments proves the superiority of Semi-supervised Hessian Eigenmap Fig. 1.

Results:

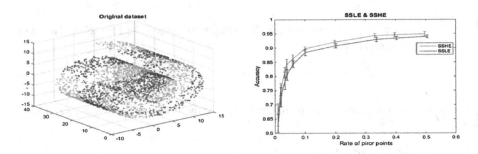

Fig. 1. Swiss Roll dataset (left) and the accuracy rates of SSLE and SSHE (right).

3.2   Experiments on MNIST

Dataset and Experiment Setting: We use the MNIST handwriting dataset which contains 60000 pictures and each picture is size of 28×28 pixels represents figure "0" to "9". For visual effects we select 800 samples for each figure from "1", "4", "7", and "9". We apply unsupervised algorithms Laplacian and Hessian Eigenmap and the derived semi-supervised techniques to this data.

Like the experiment on Swiss Roll we define the label information of supervised points who are chosen randomly as [1 0] for class one, [0 1] for class two, [−1 0] for class three and [0 −1] for class four. And we reduce the original dimensionality to 2D. Traditional unsupervised techniques Laplacian Eigenmap, Hessian Eigenmap and semi-supervised methods SSLE, SSHE are all involved in our comparison.

Results: As it is shown in Fig. 2, compared with unsupervised algorithms, semi-supervised methods divide the four classes apparently by considering only a bit of prior points. For further exploration, we increase the rate of prior data points gradually (shown in Fig. 3). Within our expectation, the boundaries of different classes become more clear and even can be classified by a linear classification with the increase of prior information. And they express the superiority of semi-supervised algorithms.

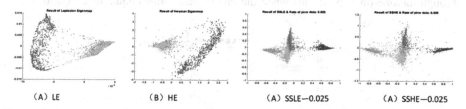

(A) LE   (B) HE   (A) SSLE−0.025   (A) SSHE−0.025

Fig. 2. The dimensionality reduction results of LE, HE, SSLE and SSHE.

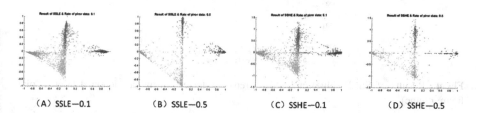

(A) SSLE−0.1   (B) SSLE−0.5   (C) SSHE−0.1   (D) SSHE−0.5

Fig. 3. The results of SSLE and SSHE with the different rate of prior points. K = 7, d = 2.

3.3   Experiments on Human Action Dataset

Dataset and Experiment Setting: We use human action dataset [11] which is achieved by 17 inertial sensors attached on different positions of the volunteers. And it contains 10 action performed by 10 people and each action with samples range from 100 to 110. The FFT feature of 3D acceleration gathered by sensors obtained through pre-process and the process including mean filter and FFT. Then we get a matrix size of 1086 × 1344 from each sensor where 1086 is the number of samples and 1334 means the dimensional coefficients of each sample. Need to say the ten categories of human actions including: jumping forward, jumping up, lying down, running, setting down, typing, walking, walking quickly and walking S.

In our experiments we extract data from partial sensors. We reduce the dimensionality to 6D and the prior data points are selected randomly, simultaneously every class contains the same rate of supervised points. We have 10 categories of human actions, so we use one hot code to represent the label information of supervised points. That means $\begin{bmatrix} 1 \underbrace{00...0}_{9} \end{bmatrix}$ corresponds to class 1, and $\begin{bmatrix} \underbrace{00...0}_{9} 1 \end{bmatrix}$ corresponds to class 10 *etc.* We increase the rate of prior points gradually from 10% to 50% and conduct experiments 10 times on each rate, then average them as the final outcomes for each condition. Representative SSLE and proposed SSHE are compared in our experiments.

Result: As it is shown in Fig. 4, with the increase of supervised spots, SSHE's performance is superior to SSLE apparently in the accuracy rate. In addition, we also find that the standard deviation of the two methods rising while the prior points reaching a certain rate. Confusion matrices of SSLE and SSHE shown in Fig. 5 are obtained through the one-off experiments when the rate of prior points equal to 25% and 50%.

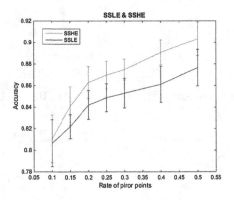

Fig. 4. Results of SSLE (blue) and SSHE (red) conducted on human action dataset. (Color figure online)

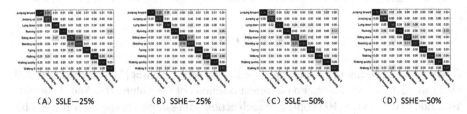

Fig. 5. Confusion matrices of SSLE and SSHE when the rate of prior points equal to 25% and 50%.

4   Conclusion

In this paper, we propose a semi-supervised Hessian Eigenmap for human action recognition. Hessian has a richer null-space and can exploit high-order information of the local geometry of data distribution. Also Hessian extrapolates nicely to unseen data.

The experimental results on both synthetic dataset and real world dataset demonstrate that the proposed semi-supervised Hessian Eigenmap algorithm outperforms the representative semi-supervised Laplacian Eigenmap algorithm.

Acknowledgement. This paper is partly supported by the National Natural Science Foundation of China (Grant Nos. 61671480, 61301242, 61271407) and the Fundamental Research Funds for the Central Universities.

References

1. Jolliffe, I.T.: Principal component analysis. Technometrics **44**(5), 594–609 (2005)
2. Wang, J.: Geometric Structure of High-Dimensional Data and Dimensionality Reduction, vol. 256, pp. 115–119. Higher Education Press/Springer, Beijing/Heidelberg (2012)
3. Roweis, S.T., Saul, L.K.: Nonlinear dimensionality reduction by locally linear embedding. Science **290**(22), 2323–2326 (2000)
4. Tenenbaum, J.B., de Silva, V., Langford, J.C.: A global geometric framework for nonlinear dimensionality reduction. Science **290**(22), 2319–2323 (2000)
5. Zhang, Z., Zha, H.: Principal manifolds and nonlinear dimension reduction via local tangent space alignment. SIAM J. Sci. Comput. **26**(1), 313–338 (2005)
6. Belkin, M., Niyogi, P.: Laplacian Eigenmaps for dimensionality reduction and data representation. Neural Comput. **15**(6), 1373–1396 (2003)
7. Donoho, D.L., Grimes, C.: Hessian Eigenmaps: new locally linear embedding techniques for high-dimensional data. PNAS **100**(10), 5591–5596 (2003)
8. Yang, X., Fu, H.Y., Zha, H.Y.: Semi-supervised nonlinear dimensionality reduction. In: Proceedings of the 23th International Conference on Machine Learning, pp. 1065–1072 (2006)
9. Hai-hong, L., Cong-hui, Z.: Semi-supervised Laplacian Eigenmap. Comput. Eng. Des. **33** (2), 601–606 (2012)
10. Kim, K.I., Steinke, F., Hein, M.: Semi-supervised regression using Hessian energy with an application to semi-supervised dimensionality reduction. In: Neural Information Processing Systems, pp. 979–987 (2009)
11. Guo, Y., Li, L., Liu, W., Cheng, J., Tao, D.: Multiview cauchy estimator feature embedding for depth and inertial sensor-based human action recognition. arXiv:1608.02183 (2016)

Surveillance Based Crowd Counting via Convolutional Neural Networks

Damin Zhang[1], Zhanming Li[1], and Pengcheng Liu[2]($\boxtimes$)

[1] College of Electrical and Information Engineering,
Lanzhou University of Technology, Lanzhou, China
zdm1992tim@163.com, lizm@lut.cn
[2] Intelligent Media Technique Research Center,
Chongqing Institute of Green and Intelligent Technology,
Chinese Academy of Sciences, Chongqing, China
liupengcheng@cigit.ac.cn

Abstract. Video surveillance based crowd counting is important for crowd management and public security. It is a challenge task due to the cluttered background, ambiguous foreground and diverse crowd distributions. In this paper, we propose an end-to-end crowd counting method with convolutional neural networks, which integrates original frames and motion cues for learning a deep crowd counting regressor. The original frames and motion cues are complementary to each other for counting the stationary and moving pedestrians. Experimental results on two widely-used crowd counting datasets demonstrate the effectiveness of our method, and achieve the state-of-the-art performance.

1 Introduction

Counting crowd pedestrians in surveillance videos draws a lot of attention because its important applications in crowd management and public security. It is especially significant for public areas with high population density. However, due to severe occlusions, diverse crowd distributions and complex background, the crowd counting in surveillance videos is a challenging problem.

Many algorithms have been proposed to count the pedestrians by detection [1–4] or trajectory-clustering [5,6]. However, these methods are limited by the severe occlusion among people in a clustered environment or in a very dense crowd. The most extensively used method for counting crowd pedestrians is feature-based regression. The traditional regressor based crowd counting methods [7–11] segment the foreground firstly, and then train regressors with hand-crafted features extracted from the foreground to predict global crowd counts. It is worth noting that segmenting the foreground target accurately in surveillance videos is a challenging task, which would significantly affect the performance of the final crowd counts prediction. In recent years, convolutional neural networks (CNN) have achieved great success in the field of computer vision. Researches [12–14] show that the features learned by the deep CNN model can explore the latent high-level semantic representation, and are more

© Springer Nature Singapore Pte Ltd. 2016
Z. Zhang and K. Huang (Eds.): IVS 2016, CCIS 664, pp. 140–146, 2016.
DOI: 10.1007/978-981-10-3476-3_17

effective than hand-crafted features for many applications. Based on the CNN framework, Zhang et al. [15] and Zhang et al. [16] proposed to regress the crowd counts of original image directly. Both of them utilize the pedestrian density map to aid the model training, and demonstrate good performance on most existing datasets. However, in order to compute the density map, the head location of every pedestrian needs to be labeled in the original image, which is time-consuming and costly.

In this paper, we propose a simple but effective surveillance based crowd counting method with the CNN framework. We learn an end-to-end crowd counting regressor with the original image frames that are only labeled with crowd counts in the training dataset. In order to alleviate the disturbance from the cluttered background, inspired by the work [17] that utilizes motion cues among video frames for crowd segmentation, we propose to integrate original and motion images for learning the crowd counting regressor. The original images are to learn some filters that are sensitive to the areas like crowd pedestrians, while the motion images are to learn some filters that focus on the foreground target. They are complementary to each other for counting the pedestrians in surveillance image frames. Extensive experiments are conducted on two commonly used crowd counting datasets, and our method achieves the state-of-the-art performance.

2   Proposed Method

The key insight of our approach is that the motion cues among video frames are beneficial to alleviate the disturbance from the cluttered background, and the original images and the corresponding motion images are complementary to each other for learning a robust deep crowd counting regressor. In the following, we will first present the process of generating the motion images, and then detail our crowd counting framework.

2.1   Motion Images Generation

Since we aim to count crowd pedestrians in surveillance videos, it would be beneficial to improve the performance of the crowd counting regressor if it is trained only with the crowd areas, but not the cluttered background, such as trees, buildings, etc. Although the crowd areas in videos are not labeled, the motion cues can help detect moving pedestrians even if they have similar textures with background, and help alleviate the cluttered background. Here, we explore the motion cues by computing motion image for each original image frame. In detail, as shown in Fig. 1, the motion images are generated by the original frames minus the mean frame of the surveillance video clip. The foreground targets are highlighted in the motion image.

Fig. 1. Pipeline of generating the motion image. Best viewed in color. (Color figure online)

2.2 Crowd Counting Model

Although the motion image is beneficial to detect the foreground targets in surveillance videos, these targets may include some other noise targets (e.g., cars, showcases, and so on) but not only the moving pedestrians. In addition, there may be some stationary crowd pedestrians in the video clips. As a consequence, we propose a deep CNN framework that integrates original and motion images for learning a robust crowd counting regressor, see Fig. 2. Here, the original image can help count the stationary pedestrians and eliminate the moving targets that are not pedestrians.

As shown in Fig. 2, our network model consists of two columns, one column for the original image while another column for the motion image. For each column, there are 5 convolutional layers and 2 fully connection layers, which are same to the configuration in the AlexNet [12]. Since the training data is limited, we change the fully connection layer **fc7** to a bottleneck layer with a lower dimensional (128-dimensional) to prevent overfitting. We merge the outputs of the two columns into one layer so that the original and motion cues are integrated. By mapping the integrated information to one fully connection layer **fc8** with 1-dimensional, we can get the prediction count of crowd pedestrians in a

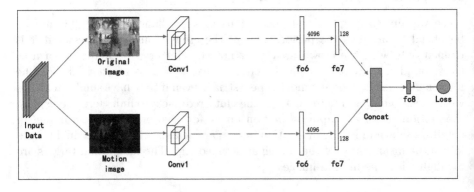

Fig. 2. The framework of our proposed method.

video frame. We place the Euclidean distance loss on the top of the **fc8** layer to directly regress the crowd count in an image frame, which is defined as follows.

$$\mathbf{F}(\theta) = \frac{1}{2N} \sum_{i=1}^{N} \|\mathbf{P}(x_i; \theta) - y_i\|^2, \tag{1}$$

where θ represents the weight parameters of our network, and $\mathbf{P}(x_i; \theta)$ outputs the prediction count of frame x_i while y_i is the corresponding ground truth crowd count.

The loss function is optimized via batch-based stochastic gradient descent and backpropagation. Since the number of training samples are very limited, the layers before **fc7** in each column are initialized by the AlexNet model [12] trained on ImageNet, and their learning rates are set to 0. We firstly pretrain CNN in each column separately by directly mapping the output of **fc7** to **fc8**. Then we utilize the pretrained CNNs to initial the two columns in our final model and fine-tune the parameters in **fc7** and **fc8** layers.

3   Experiments

We evaluate our method on two widely-used crowd counting benchmarks. Experimental results demonstrate the effectiveness of our method, and achieve the state-of-the-art performance on both datasets. Implementation of the proposed network is based on the Caffe framework developed by [18]. In the following, we will first explain the evaluation metric, and then we introduce the two benchmark datasets. Finally, the experimental results are presented.

3.1   Evaluation Metric

By following the convention of previous work [7,15,19] for crowd counting, we evaluate different methods with three kinds of evaluation metric: mean average precision (MAP), mean average error (MAE) and mean square error (MSE). They are defined as follows:

$$MAP = 1 - \frac{1}{N} \sum_{i=1}^{N} \frac{|\tilde{y}_i - y_i|}{y_i}, MAE = \frac{1}{N} \sum_{i=1}^{N} |\tilde{y}_i - y_i|, MSE = \frac{1}{N} \sum_{i=1}^{N} (\tilde{y}_i - y_i)^2,$$

where N is the number of test images, $\tilde{y}_i$ is the predicted pedestrian count of the ith image frame, and y_i is the ground truth pedestrian count of the ith image frame. Roughly speaking, MAP and MAE indicate the accuracy of the learned model, and MSE indicates the robustness of the learned model.

3.2   Datasets

For the research of crowd counting, there are two most widely-used datasets: UCSD [7] and Mall [9]. Example frames of the two datasets are shown in Fig. 3.

Fig. 3. Example frames of the datasets. (a) UCSD dataset. (b) Mall dataset.

- **UCSD:** It contains 2000 frames chosen from one surveillance camera on UCSD campus walkways. The frame size is 158×238. There are about 25 persons on average in each frame. By following the same setting with previous work [7,15], we use frames from 601 to 1400 as training samples, and the remaining 1200 frames are used as test data.
- **Mall:** It is a dataset collected from a publicly accessible webcam in a mall for crowd counting. There are over 60,000 pedestrians were labeled in 2000 video frames. The frame size is 480×640. We adopt the same experimental setting with [9], the first 800 frames are selected as training data, and the rest 1200 frames are selected as test data.

3.3 Results

We first verify the effectiveness of merging the original and motion cues for crowd counting based on the Mall dataset. The results are shown in Table 1. Comparing to the CNN network with only the original images as input, the MAP of crowd counting is improved by integrating the original and motion information for learning the crowd counting regressor. This demonstrates the effectiveness of merging the original and motion cues for crowd counting in some degree.

Table 1. Experimental results on the Mall dataset with different input information

Method	MAP
Only original image	0.91
Original and motion images	0.92

We also compare our method with other popular regression based crowd counting methods. The experimental results are shown in Table 2. Most of the methods learn the crowd counting regressor based on the hand-crafted features, except the cross-scene crowd counting [15] and our methods utilize the deep CNN features. From the results in Table 2, we can see that the CNN network based methods show better crowd counting performance (the smaller, the better), especially on the UCSD dataset. Our baseline is the output of our model trained only

Table 2. Comparision results in UCSD and Mall datasets

Method	UCSD		Mall	
	MAE	MSE	MAE	MSE
Kernel ridge regression [20]	2.16	7.45	-	-
Ridge regression [19]	2.25	7.82	3.59	19.00
Texture analysis counting [21]	2.60	10.1	3.90	23.90
Gaussian process regression [7]	2.24	7.97	3.72	20.10
Multiple output regression [9]	2.29	8.08	3.15	15.70
Cross-scene crowd counting [15]	1.60	**3.31**	-	-
Our baseline	1.76	6.56	3.24	15.58
Our method	**1.53**	3.76	**3.09**	**15.22**

with the original images. The performance of our baseline is comparable with the cross-scene crowd counting method [15], even though they used extra pedestrian head location information. By integrating the motion cues into our baseline, our final method shows the best results on both datasets. This again validates the effectiveness of our method that integrates the original and motion images for crowd counting.

4 Conclusion

In this paper, we propose an end-to-end surveillance based crowd counting method with the CNN framework. In order to count the stationary and moving pedestrians effectively, we integrate the original frames and motion cues for learning a robust deep crowd counting regressor. Experimental results on the widely-used UCSD and Mall datasets show that the proposed method is effective for surveillance based crowd counting, and achieve the best results on both datasets.

Acknowledgment. This work is funded by the National Natural Science Foundation of China (Grant No. 61602433 and Grant No. 61472386), and the Strategic Priority Research Program of the Chinese Academy of Sciences (Grant XDA06040103). The two Titan X GPUs used for this research were donated by the NVIDIA Corporation.

References

1. Wu, B., Nevatia, R.: Detection of multiple, partially occluded humans in a single image by Bayesian combination of edgelet part detectors. In: ICCV (2005)
2. Li, M., Zhang, Z., Huang, K., Tan, T.: Estimating the number of people in crowded scenes by MID based foreground segmentation and head-shoulder detection. In: ICPR (2008)
3. Wang, M., Wang, X.: Automatic adaptation of a generic pedestrian detector to a specific traffic scene. In: CVPR (2011)

4. Lin, Z., Davis, L.S.: Shape-based human detection and segmentation via hierarchical part-template matching. IEEE Trans. Pattern Anal. Mach. Intell. **32**, 604–618 (2010)
5. Rabaud, V., Belongie, S.: Counting crowded moving objects. In: CVPR (2006)
6. Brostow, G.J., Cipolla, R.: Unsupervised Bayesian detection of independent motion in crowds. In: CVPR (2006)
7. Chan, A.B., Liang, Z.S.J., Vasconcelos, N.: Privacy preserving crowd monitoring: counting people without people models or tracking. In: CVPR (2008)
8. Chan, A.B., Vasconcelos, N.: Bayesian poisson regression for crowd counting. In: ICCV (2009)
9. Chen, K., Loy, C.C., Gong, S., Xiang, T.: Feature mining for localised crowd counting. In: BMVC (2012)
10. Chen, K., Gong, S., Xiang, T., Mary, Q., Loy, C.C.: Cumulative attribute space for age and crowd density estimation. In: CVPR (2013)
11. Liu, B., Vasconcelos, N.: Bayesian model adaptation for crowd counts. In: ICCV (2015)
12. Krizhevsky, A., Sutskever, I., Hinton, G.E.: Imagenet classification with deep convolutional neural networks. In: NIPS (2012)
13. Sermanet, P., Eigen, D., Zhang, X., Mathieu, M., Fergus, R., LeCun, Y.: Overfeat: integrated recognition, localization and detection using convolutional networks. arXiv:1312.6229 (2013)
14. Donahue, J., Jia, Y., Vinyals, O., Hoffman, J., Zhang, N., Tzeng, E., Darrell, T.: DeCAF: a deep convolutional activation feature for generic visual recognition. In: ICML (2014)
15. Zhang, C., Li, H., Wang, X., Yang, X.: Cross-scene crowd counting via deep convolutional neural networks. In: CVPR (2015)
16. Zhang, Y., Zhou, D., Chen, S., Gao, S., Ma, Y.: Single-image crowd counting via multi-column convolutional neural network. In: CVPR (2016)
17. Kang, K., Wang, X.: Fully convolutional neural networks for crowd segmentation. arXiv:1411.4464 (2014)
18. Jia, Y., Shelhamer, E., Donahue, J., Karayev, S., Long, J., Girshick, R., Guadarrama, S., Darrell, T.: Caffe: Convolutional architecture for fast feature embedding. arXiv:1408.5093 (2014)
19. Saunders, C., Gammerman, A., Vvovk, V.: Ridge regression learning algorithm in dual variables. In: ICML (2015)
20. An, S., Liu, W., Venkatesh, S.: Face recognition using kernel ridge regression. In: CVPR (2007)
21. Wu, X., Liang, G., Lee, K.K., Xu, Y.: Crowd density estimation using texture analysis and learning. In: IEEE International Conference on Robotics and Biomimetics (2006)

Jet Trajectory Recognition Based on Dark Channel Prior

Wenyan Chong, Ying Hu[✉], Defei Yuan, and Yongjun Ma

Automation Research Center, Dalian Maritime University, Dalian 116026, China
huying@dlmu.edu.cn

Abstract. The automatic fire-fighting water cannon is an important device for fire extinguish. By identifying the jet trajectory, the closed-loop control of fire extinguishing process can be realized, which improves the quality and efficiency of the water cannon. In this paper, a novel jet trajectory recognition method based on the dark channel prior and the optical properties of low scene transmission in the jet trajectory's coverage area is proposed. Firstly, the dark channel prior was used to extract the low scene transmission region. Then, in order to identify the jet trajectory more accurately, this extracted region was matched with the moving target area which is restored by Gaussian mixture background modeling. Finally, the modified cubic curve is used to fit out jet trajectory and predict its ending. The experimental results indicate that the proposed approach can effectively detect the jet trajectory with strong anti-interference ability and higher accuracy.

Keywords: Fire-fighting water cannon · Jet trajectory recognition · Dark channel prior · Curve fitting · Gaussian mixture modeling

1 Introduction

Nowadays, the fire disaster has become a serious threat to human survival and development. It is urgent to improve the effect of the fire extinguishing equipment. So the research on closed-loop control fire-fighting water cannon which focused on the jet trajectory recognition has become a hotspot in recent years.

There have been many related work about the jet trajectory recognition. Feng et al. [1] derived the beam equation of the jet trajectory based on the exterior ballistics and the particle kinematics. Jing [2] proposed a segmentation algorithm based on the improved OTSU approach and region growing for the jet trajectory. An extraction algorithm for the jet trajectory in colorful pictures based on the difference of RGB was presented by Weilu and Min [3]. A Multi-trajectory Vector Search Method (MTVSM) was proposed by Jie et al. [4], which is used to extract feature points in the jet trajectory. In addition, as for the multi-starting points search method of the jet trajectory, Guo [5] proposed the diagonal line method. Hao [6] put forward a stepwise filtering optimization method based on the fitness of Particle Swarm Optimization (PSO) [7].

In the above researches, the essence of the preliminary extraction of the jet trajectory is based on the background subtraction and the dynamic, static characteristics of

© Springer Nature Singapore Pte Ltd. 2016
Z. Zhang and K. Huang (Eds.): IVS 2016, CCIS 664, pp. 147–153, 2016.
DOI: 10.1007/978-981-10-3476-3_18

the jet trajectory. Some interference is unable to exclude, such as the changing ambient light, high brightness background, moving objects, water stains, and the bifurcation of the jet caused by the air resistance and other reasons. To address these problems, a novel jet trajectory recognition method based on the dark channel prior is proposed in this paper. That can overcome the above defects, improve the recognition accuracy and do a good groundwork for the closed-loop control of the water cannon.

2 Jet Region Recognition

2.1 Low Scene Transmission Region Extraction

Dark Channel Prior. In the jet image, because there are a large amounts of water droplets in the jet coverage area form scattering, this effect is similar to other suspended particles in natural haze image. Therefore, the dark channel prior theory in haze image proposed by He et al. [8] in CVPR can be applied to the jet trajectory recognition. The prior said, any haze-free image except the sky always exists some pixels that have lower intensities in at least one channel of the RGB color space (dark channel):

$$J_{\text{dark}}(x) = \min_{c \in \{r,g,b\}} \left(\min_{y \in \Omega(x)} (J^c(y)) \right) \approx I_b(x) = \int_0^d A\beta e^{-\beta d(x)} dx = (1 - e^{-\beta d(x)})A \quad (1)$$

From (1) we know:

$$t(x) = e^{-\beta d(x)} = 1 - \frac{I_b}{A} \quad (2)$$

Where $t(x)$ is the scene transmission that describes how light transfers in the atmosphere, and $0 \le t(x) \le 1$. The intensity of $J_{dark}(x)$ which is used the blackbody radiation model to approximate is lowest in the dark channel and tends to zero, $t(x) \to 1$. It means that the scene transmission in the dark channel is quite high. Yang et al. [9] presented that the suspended particles are smaller, the impact on the image is relatively small, the atmospheric transmission is commonly $t(x) = 0.8$ under normal conditions. It is in line with the dark channel prior.

But He et al. [8] also presented that the dark channel prior exists limitations. What's more, the limitations are used to identify and remove the haze area which is not in conformity with the dark channel prior theory [10]. The concrete embodiment of the limitations in the jet images is that some regions do not exist the dark channel (do not meet the dark channel prior formula (1)) such as the jet trajectory and the white walls, water stains, and other interference which is very similar to the air light. The patch $\Omega(x)$ was used to traverse these areas, you would find it has the characteristics (Fig. 1):

$$J_{\text{dark}}(x) = \min_{c \in \{r,g,b\}} (\min_{y \in \Omega(x)} (J^c(y))) \rightarrow 1 \ t(x) \rightarrow 0 \qquad (3)$$

The scene transmission $t(x) \rightarrow 0$ could be described as the low scene transmission region. This paper also used this limitation of the dark channel prior combined with the scene transmission formula (2) to extract the jet region in Fig. 2. Because this grayscale image is not conducive to the follow-up work, so the OTSU is used to get the binary transmission image shown in Fig. 3. Fortunately, the interference in these areas is not motion region except for the jet region, so it could be removed by the subsequent image matching with motion region. It not only can extract the jet region, but also remove the moving object and other interference which is introduced by background subtraction.

Fig. 1. Original image on angle 1

Fig. 2. Transmission image

Fig. 3. Binary transmission image

2.2   Motion Region Identification

Gaussian Mixture Modeling (GMM) and Background Updating. Besides the optical properties of the low scene transmission, the jet trajectory also has the motion characteristics, so it can also adopt moving object extraction method at the same time to extract the jet trajectory initially. Because GMM is one of the best models for modeling a background scene with gradual changes and repetitive motions [11]. While in the jet images the changes of the illumination, water stains and other interference are gradual, so GMM is suitable for the jet trajectory extraction. The principle of the GMM is that each pixel of the change of RGB values of three-channel respectively can be described by a mixture of K Gaussian distributions at time t:

$$P(X_t) = \sum_{K=1}^{K} W_{k,t} \bullet \eta\left(X_t, u_{k,t}, \sum k, t\right) \qquad (4)$$

Where each pixel color is presented with a random variable X, probability of the observed value is Xt, K is the number of Gaussian distributions, wk, t is the weight-iness of the kth Gaussian distribution at time t, $\eta(X_t, u_{k,t}, \sum k, t)$ is the Gaussian probability density function. Where u_t is the mean, n is the channel number, the covariance matrix can be described as $\sum k, t = \sigma_t^2 \bullet I$. Where σ_t^2 is standard deviation.

Because of the interference such as the changing ambient light exists, the fixed background could not adapt to the small changes in the scene, the background updating should be carried on [11]. The update rules of background modeling as follows:

$$\alpha_t = (1 - \rho)\alpha_{t-1}^2 + \rho(X_t - u_t)^T(X_t - u_t) \tag{5}$$

2.3   Image Matching

Through the above steps, we have gotten the transmission image in Fig. 3 and the motion region image after morphology filtering [12] in Fig. 4. The next step is matching (and operations) the two figures to get the matching image in Fig. 5. This matching image excludes the white walls, water stains, bright sunlight windows and other interference which is similar to the air light in the low scene transmission image, and the interference of changing ambient light, moving objects in the motion region image, only retains the motion region with the low transmission of jet trajectory in Fig. 5.

Fig. 4. Extracted motion region

Fig. 5. Jet region after matching

3   Jet Trajectory Identification

3.1   Feature Point Extraction

Based on the jet region recognition, the rough regions of the jet trajectory have been identified. But because of the influence of air resistance, the extracted main jet trajectory is not clear enough, with the interference of the scattered clouds of spray in the rear section. Meanwhile, due to the defects in image processing, the cutoff parts were existed in the jet region, so the jet trajectory can't be identified accurately. Therefore, this paper takes the vertical search method [13] to extract the feature points in Fig. 6.

3.2   Jet Trajectory Fitting

Though the above operation, the jet region and the feature points of the jet trajectory were extracted, then the curve is used to fit the jet trajectory and predict the jet ending. The actual water cannons have the traits of high speed, high water pressure. Therefore, the jet trajectory in the early stage keeps the good water type only affected by the gravity

Fig. 6. Feature points extraction of jet trajectory (Color figure online)

Fig. 7. Fitting curve of jet trajectory (Color figure online)

and presents the ideal parabola. In the late stage, the curve of the jet trajectory would appear bifurcation and deformation affected by the air resistance and fluid dynamics, so the later stages of the jet need to forecast. This paper has tried to use the least squares fitting parabolic [14] (blue curve), cubic curve (red curve) and the piecewise weighted cubic curve (green curve) to predict the jet according to its morphological properties in Fig. 7. In the end, the piecewise weighted cubic curve was chosen to fit out the jet trajectory, because it is better consistent with the actual jet than others.

4 Results and Analysis

Interference test is done on the jet trajectory recognition in the next two experiments.

The interference in the first set of experiments is the strong light by changing the shooting angle. Some sunshine through the window shoot onto the jet image, so only using the traditional method based on the motion characteristics of the jet trajectory would introduce some interference of the jump spot (Fig. 8(g)). While these interference can be filtered out in this paper. Because these regions are belonged to the dark channel in the transmission image, the interference is basically removed in the matching image (Fig. 9).

(a) original image (b) transmission image (c) matching image(d)feature points extraction

(e) jet fitting (f)location of the water points (g)the traditional method for jet region extraction

Fig. 8. Interference test of the changing ambient light in the jet trajectory on angle 2 (Color figure online)

(a)original image (b) matching image(c)fitting curve (d)the traditional method for jet extraction

Fig. 9. Interference test of bifurcation of the jet in the jet trajectory on angle 3 (Color figure online)

The interference in the second is the bifurcation of the terminal jet trajectory affected by air resistance, the traditional method would introduce some water mist interference. The above interference makes it difficult to extract the feature point and fit the curve. But these interference regions are also belonged to the dark channel which could be removed by matching and the main part of the jet trajectory could be clearly to extract.

5   Conclusions

The experimental results prove that this algorithm can identify the jet trajectory accurately and completely even under the complex conditions. It has strong robustness and high detection rate. It is significant for positioning of the jet ending, realizing closed loop control of the water cannon and other subsequent research.

Acknowledgment. This work is supported by the China Fundamental Research Funds for the Central Universities, No: 3132016025.

References

1. Feng, W., Xiaoyang, C., et al.: Fitting equation of the monitor's jet track. Fire Sci. Technol. **26**(6), 656–658 (2007). (in Chinese)
2. Jing, C.: Image segmentation and recognition algorithm for the fire cannon's jet trajectory. Electron. Sci. Technol. **23**(3), 43–49 (2010). (in Chinese)
3. Weilu, S., Min, Z.: The extraction algorithm for the fire cannon's jet trajectory in colorful pictures. Electron. Sci. Technol. **24**(3), 27–37 (2011). (in Chinese)
4. Jie, Y., Min, Z., Liang, L., et al.: Jet trajectory recognition method based on multi-trajectory vecter search. Comput. Eng. **41**(7), 280–284 (2015). (in Chinese)
5. Guo, X.: Image processing and fire control software design in intelligent fire fighting system. Nanjing University of Aeronautics and Astronautics, pp. 22–30 (2011). (in Chinese)
6. Hao, S.: Stepwise selection method of fire-fighting cannon trajectory. Mach. Build. Autom. **44**(1), 217–219 (2015). (in Chinese)
7. Yanmin, L., Qingzhen, Z.: Research of particle swarm optimization and its application. Shandong Normal University (2011)

8. He, K., Sun, J., Tang, X.: Single image haze removal using dark channel prior. IEEE Trans. Pattern Anal. Mach. Intell. **33**(12), 2341–2353 (2011)
9. Yang, H., Liu, X.P., Guo, Y.: Influence of atmosphere to space camera's image. Spacecr. Recovery Remote Sens. **29**(2), 18–22 (2008). (in Chinese)
10. Shuai, F., Yong, W., Yang, C., et al.: Restoration of image degraded by haze. Acta Electron. Sin. **10**(38), 2279–2284 (2010). (in Chinese)
11. Zhu, Y., Fujimura, K.: Driver face tracking using Gaussian mixture model (GMM) (2003)
12. Yujin, Z.: Image Processing, 3rd edn, pp. 107–114. Tsinghua University Press, Beijing (2012). (in Chinese)
13. Jing, C.: Research on automatic orientation of fire-fighting monitor based on image processing. Nanjing University of Aeronautics and Astronautics (2010). (in Chinese)
14. Liangbo, C., Yaqing, Z.: Study on curve fitting based on least square method. J. Wuxi Inst. Technol. **11**(5), 52–55 (2012)

Real-Time Abnormal Behavior Detection in Elevator

Yujie Zhu[1,2(✉)] and Zengfu Wang[1,2(✉)]

[1] Institute of Intelligent Machines, Hefei Institutes of Physical Sciences,
Chinese Academy of Sciences, Hefei, China
[2] University of Science and Technology of China, Hefei, China
zhuyj@mail.ustc.edu.cn, zfwang@ustc.edu.cn

Abstract. Violent behaviors occurred in elevators have been frequently reported by media in recent years. It is necessary to provide a safe elevator environment for passengers. A new visual surveillance system with the function of abnormal behavior detection is proposed in this paper. Firstly, human objects in surveillance video are extracted by background subtraction, and meanwhile the number of people in each image is counted. Then, some algorithms are presented to deal with different abnormal behaviors. For one person case, we pay attention to whether the person fell down or not. And for two or more people case, we use the image entropy of Motion History Image (MHI) to detect if there is violent behavior. Experimental results show that the proposed algorithms can offer satisfactory results.

1 Introduction

There is a gradually wide spread use of elevators in high-rise buildings as the progress of industrial technology. While several criminal behavior events taking place in the elevator have been reported recently, including robbery, kidnapping, violence and so on. It's urgent to provide a safe and advanced vehicle for passengers. Traditional surveillance system is installed to monitor what happens in an elevator. However it is extremely tedious to search for violent behaviors with a very low probability. While there have been increasing efforts to tackle this problem, it remains rather challenging due to compound issue such as occluding, camouflage, illumination changes, tracking failure, video noise and so on.

Human action recognition and behavior detection draw a lot of attention in computer vision. In recent years, many algorithms have been proposed to improve interest point detection, local spatio-temporal descriptors, and building relationships among local features [1]. Most of the algorithms focus on single action, such as hand-waving, running, or horse riding. The work mentioned above does not consider abnormal event detection among multiple people.

Several algorithms for abnormal detection have been proposed in recent years. Adam et al. [2] monitor low-level measurements in a set of fixed spatial positions and integral-pixel approximations of optical flow to detect usual event. Mehran et al. [3] place a grid of particles over the image and treat the moving particles

© Springer Nature Singapore Pte Ltd. 2016
Z. Zhang and K. Huang (Eds.): IVS 2016, CCIS 664, pp. 154–161, 2016.
DOI: 10.1007/978-981-10-3476-3_19

as individuals which are drawn by the space-time average of optical. Abnormal behavior is detected using social force model. Cui et al. [4] propose an interaction energy potential function to represent the current behavior state of a subject. However these methods are focused on crowed movement in public place, which can't handle the scene where people in a confined place.

In the real world, the definitions of abnormal behavior of person are various in different scenes. For example, it's normal for a person exercising on square, which will be treated as strange on the contrary in classroom. Thus there isn't a unified standard to define anomalies. One common solution is to see the event deviating from the expect as abnormal behavior according to the specific situation.

In our work, we define failing down as an abnormal behavior while there is only one passenger in elevator. When there are more than one passengers in elevator, fighting with each other is considered as abnormal.

Our characteristics are summarized as below. (1) Our method does not rely on human tracking, so it is more robust to errors that are introduced by tracking failure. (2) We just only detect motion information which is the precondition for violent behavior. (3) We do not extract angular point or calculate optical flow, thus the algorithm is with less complex calculation.

2 Our Approach

The framework of this paper is summarized in Fig. 1. We firstly extract human objects and count the number of people. And then different abnormal behavior detection algorithms are designed according to the number of passengers in elevator.

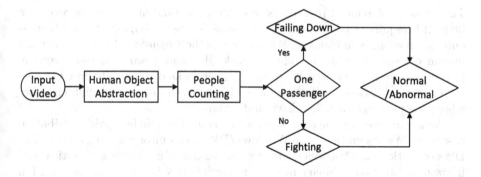

Fig. 1. Flow chart.

2.1 Human Body Object Extraction and People Counting

It is convenient to extract human objects by background subtraction, for the background of the scene in an elevator is static and simple. The accuracy of the result is mainly influenced by the variation of illumination intensity. We adopt the statical method proposed by Horprasert et al. in [5], which achieves outstanding results in shadow detection. Different from [5], we classify a pixel to be part of human object foreground or background including shaded background, shadow and highlight background. Finally, human object foreground is acquired by applying morphology operation on the raw mask.

People counting is necessary to decide how to detect abnormal behavior, because the possible abnormal behaviors will be different according to the number of people. It is effective to count the number of passengers by calculating connected region pixels when there is no serious occlusion between people. The result of people counting is shown in Fig. 2.

Fig. 2. The result of human objects abstraction and people counting.

2.2 Single People Detection

The normal behavior of passengers in elevator is stand-up or moving around a little. It is required to detect whether someone is failed down or not when there is only one passenger in elevator. We use the method mentioned above to extract human objects and obtain a binary mask. Horizontal projection and vertical projections are implemented on the mask. There is an obvious difference between vertical and horizontal projections of the binary masks of the two different cases where one passenger is failed down and stand-up.

We are inspired by the idea of [6], which counts people by a grid distribution of sensors. We design Detection Windows (DW) to monitor what is going on. The DWs of vertical and horizontal are interest regions of projections of vertical and horizontal direction of binary mask. The vertical DW is taken from one third of the original window of the vertical direction projection from left side. Similarly, the horizontal DW is taken from bottom. It will be masked to be active if the DW has more than 65% nonzero pixels. On the contrary, the DW will be seen as inactive.

We can judge the status of the passenger in elevator by monitoring the condition of the two DWs of vertical and horizontal direction. If the vertical DW is active and the horizontal DW is inactive, we infer the passenger is stand-up.

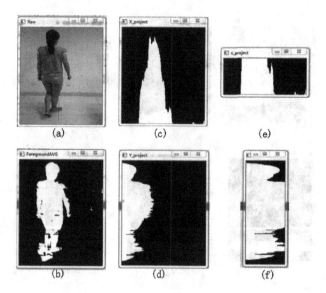

Fig. 3. (a) The input raw frame of standing up. (b) The binary mask obtained by background subtraction. (c) The horizontal projection of the binary mask. (d) The vertical projection of the binary mask. (e) The detection window of horizontal direction. (f) The detection window of vertical direction.

Otherwise it's considered that the passenger is failed down when the vertical DW is inactive and the horizontal DW is active.

The horizontal projection and vertical projections of normal case of standing up and abnormal case of failing down are shown as Figs. 3 and 4. The original input frames and the binary masks derived by background subtraction are shown in Figs. 3(a), 4(a) and Figs. 3(b), 4(b) separately. The horizontal and vertical direction projections of the binary masks are exhibited in Figs. 3(c), 4(c) and Figs. 3(d), 4(d) separately. Figures 3(e), 4(e) and Figs. 3(f), 4(f) are DWs of horizontal direction and vertical direction. For Fig. 3 the DWs of vertical and horizontal direction are active and inactive respectively, from which we consider the passenger is stand-up. For Fig. 4 the DWs of vertical and horizontal direction are inactive and active separately, from which it can be considered that the passenger is failed down.

2.3 More Than One People Detection

The behaviors of human in elevator is limited. Most of the people stand alone hardly moving around or doing some kinds of complex action in the narrow space, in contrast to in other scenes, such as plaza, railway station, outdoors and so on. The peace will be broken when violent behaviors take place. Thus we are inspired to extract movement, which is the necessary requirement for the occurrence of abnormal behavior. We intend to tackle this issue by detecting motion and expressing motion from the aspect of energy function.

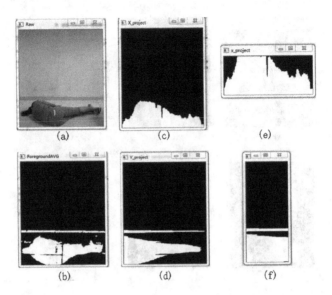

Fig. 4. (a) The input raw frame of failing down. (b) The binary mask obtained by background subtraction. (c) The horizontal projection of the binary mask. (d) The vertical projection of the binary mask. (e) The detection window of horizontal direction. (f) The detection window of vertical direction.

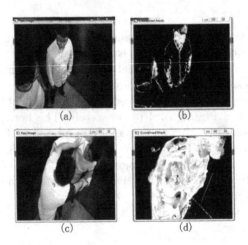

Fig. 5. (a) and (c) are input fames. (b) and (d) are corresponding MHIs.

We express motion by Motion History Image [7]. The MHIs of standing still and fighting are shown in Fig. 5(b) and (d). The brighter pixels denote more recent motion and the gray darker pixels indicate earlier motion.

Information entropy is used in image, called image entropy, to depict the amount of information of an image. We can see from Fig. 5(b) and (d), the nonzero pixels of the two cases are different remarkably. The entropies of the two image will also be greatly different. We improve the calculation formula of one dimensional entropy of gray image as

$$E = - \sum_{i=0}^{255} (i/255)\, p(i) \log_2 p(i) \;.$$ (1)

The gray image entropy mention in (1) is seen as weighted entropy that means to assign a great weight to recent motion. The weighted entropy is used as energy function to distinguish abnormal behavior such as fighting with high energy. Average value μ and standard deviation σ of energy function are calculated by T successive frames of normal cases. The discriminant function of the current frame is shown as

$$discriminant\ \ result = \begin{cases} normal & if\ \left|\frac{E-u}{\sigma}\right| \leq \lambda \\ abnormal & if\ \left|\frac{E-u}{\sigma}\right| \gg \lambda \end{cases}.$$ (2)

In Eq. (2) λ is determined empirically.

3   Experimental Results

The data sets of elevator monitoring videos are collected by the research team. The fighting and failing down videos are recorded by Panasonic HDC-HS20 digital video. The experiment environment of hardware is desktop computer with 3.60 GHz Intel(R) Core(TM) i7-4790 CPU, 8G RAM. The softwares are Visual Studio 2013 and Opencv2.4.10 on Windows 7 operation system.

3.1   One People Detection

The initial frames for background subtraction is static background without person. The number of initial frames is 25. The algorithm is tested on 4 segment videos. The size of each frame is 320 × 640. The accuracy of the algorithm proposed in this paper is shown in Table 1. We also compare our algorithm with the contour matching method in literature [8], the correct rate and processing speed are shown in Table 2.

Table 1. The accuracy of falling down detection.

Test videos	The total number of frames	Accuracy of detection
video1	761	92.35%
video2	721	92.29%
video3	743	92.54%
video4	811	92.72%

Table 2. The comparison of results of falling down detection with another method [8].

Algorithm	Accuracy of detection	Processing time of per frame
Contour matching	91.00%	0.0274
Algorithm in this paper	92.54%	0.0203

3.2 More Than One People Detection

In our experiment, we select $\lambda = 5$ by trial and error and T = 60. The average entropy of normal case is $\mu = 11.48$ and the standard deviation is $\sigma = 0.8276$. The result of experiment is shown in Fig. 6. It can be seen that the image entropies are between 0 and 20 when the passengers are standing still or moving a little. The entropy will increase sharply when there is violent behavior. The 155th frame begin to increase dramatically. The comparison experiment with the setting threshold method in literature [9] is shown in Table 3.

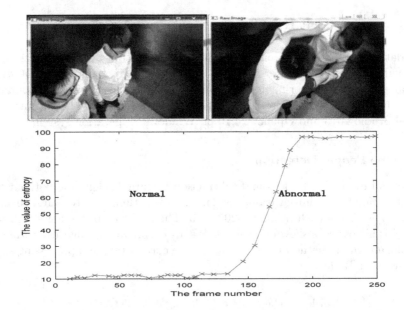

Fig. 6. The result of more than one people abnormal behavior detection.

Table 3. The comparison of results of violent behavior with another method [9].

Algorithm	Accuracy of detection	Processing frames of per second
Threshold comparison	84.00%	25
Algorithm in this paper	92.54%	27

4   Conclusion

We propose a new visual surveillance system with the function of abnormal behavior detection in elevator. Human objects in surveillance video are extracted by background subtraction, and meanwhile the number of people in each frame is counted. Different abnormal detection methods are designed according to the number of passengers. Detection window and improved image entropy which is seen as energy function are exploited to detect abnormal behavior. The experiments show that our formula offers content results in elevator scenes. The algorithm mentioned in this paper not only provides high detection accuracy but also with low computation complexity. What's more it can run in real time. However there is a limitation on the number of passengers. When there are too many passengers in elevator, the detection accuracy will decrease because of occlusion. We will try to solve this problem in future.

References

1. Sun, J., Wu, X., Yan, S., Cheong, L.F., Chua, T.S., Li, J.: Hierarchical spatio-temporal context modeling for action recognition. In: IEEE Conference on CVPR 2009, pp. 2004–2011 (2009)
2. Adam, A., Rivlin, E., Shimshoni, I., et al.: Robust real-time unusual event detection using multiple fixed-location monitors. IEEE Trans. Pattern Anal. Mach. Intell. **30**(3), 555–560 (2008)
3. Mehran, R., Oyama, A., Shah, M.: Abnormal crowd behavior detection using social force model. In: IEEE Conference on Computer Vision and Pattern Recognition, pp. 935–942 (2009)
4. Cui, X., Liu, Q., Gao, M., Metaxas, D.N.: Abnormal detection using interaction energy potentials. In: 2011 IEEE Conference on Computer Vision and Pattern Recognition (CVPR), pp. 3161–3167 (2011)
5. Horprasert, T., Harwood, D., Davis, L.S.: A statistical approach for real-time robust background subtraction and shadow detection. In: IEEE ICCV, vol. 99 (1999)
6. Del Pizzo, L., et al.: Counting people by RGB or depth overhead cameras. Pattern Recogn. Lett. **81**, 41–50 (2016)
7. Ahad, M.A.R., Tan, J.K., Kim, H., Ishikawa, S.: Motion history image: its variants and applications. Mach. Vis. Appl. **23**(2), 255–281 (2012)
8. Fu, G.J., Shu, G.: Research on abnormal behavior recognition in the elevator. Harbin University of Science and Technology, Harbin, pp. 43–47 (2015)
9. Tang, Y.P., Lu, H.F.: The elevator violence prevention based on computer vision intelligent video surveillance. J. ZheJiang Univ. Technol. **37**(6), 15–19 (2009)

Author Index

Printed in the United States
By Bookmasters